T0355975

I Am Unemployed ...
Now What Do I Do?

An Organized Approach to Becoming Employed

Wayne L. Anderson
Executive Leadership Coach

iUniverse, Inc.
Bloomington

I Am Unemployed ... Now What Do I Do?
An Organized Approach to Becoming Employed

iUniverse books may be ordered through booksellers or by contacting:

iUniverse
1663 Liberty Drive
Bloomington, IN 47403
www.iuniverse.com
1-800-Authors (1-800-288-4677)

Because of the dynamic nature of the Internet, any Web addresses or links contained in this book may have changed since publication and may no longer be valid. The views expressed in this work are solely those of the author and do not necessarily reflect the views of the publisher, and the publisher hereby disclaims any responsibility for them.

Any people depicted in stock imagery provided by Thinkstock are models, and such images are being used for illustrative purposes only.

Certain stock imagery © Thinkstock.

ISBN: 978-1-4620-0642-7 (pbk)
ISBN: 978-1-4620-0643-4 (cloth)
ISBN: 978-1-4620-0644-1 (ebk)

Printed in the United States of America

iUniverse rev. date: 5/31/2011

*Anything the human mind can conceive
and believe it can achieve.*

—Napoleon Hill

I dedicate this book to the many people who are out of work for whatever reason but have refused to give up. These professionals are required to look for work in a world that is changing at an exceptionally rapid rate. They are among the many professionals who are devoted to their families, their professions, and their industries. They are the dedicated people who have transformed many companies from small shops to major corporate players in the fiercely competitive business landscape. Their efforts have been rewarded with the opportunity to seek employment somewhere else.

Acknowledgments

I want to thank my wife, Pam, who played the role of subject-matter expert, editor, consultant—and sometimes, conscience. She provided a great deal of encouragement and support during the creation of the manuscript.

In addition, a book like this could never have come to fruition without the help of a large number of people. The many job seekers with whom I have worked over the years have provided me with the experiences and inspiration that form the basis of this book.

Contents

Preface

I was laid off when I was a senior vice president at a $2.6 billion travel distribution company with close to a thousand people in my organization. This was the third time that I had been laid off from a senior management position. Your immediate thought is probably that I was a poor performer or, at minimum, had trouble doing my job. To the contrary, I was considered a top performer, earned the highest ratings available, received numerous large bonuses and generous stock options, and consistently met or outperformed my operational metrics.

So what happened?

The first layoff had to do with a company merger. It was a merger of equals. Unfortunately, our management team was not as equal as the other company's management team. The following two layoffs were due to corporate downsizing. They were not a result of any recessionary problems. In one case, the company simply outsourced almost half of its business. This left a large number of high-level management people with relatively small departments to manage.

My point in telling you this is to make sure you understand that being out of work in many cases has little to do with how good you were at your job. There are a variety of reasons why people get laid off, including an economic recession. It is almost *fashionable* to be laid off at least once. As of this writing, the United States has an unemployment rate of about 10 percent. This means there are 15.3 million people out of work. This is due to the recession that began over a year and a half ago. I am convinced that most of the people who are out of work are good at what they do for a living; losing their jobs was totally out of their control. So, then the question is not whether you will be laid off, but, "What will you do about it when it happens?"

I was devastated the first time I was laid off. I could not believe that my company would do such a thing to a loyal employee who had received such good performance reviews. After about a month of complete inaction following the layoff, I decided one day to take a good look at myself. I assessed all of my skills, not just the ones that I had used for my previous job. As an executive, one of the skills that I had developed over the years was strategic planning, a series of techniques that companies use to sell their products in the marketplace. So I decided to adjust those techniques in order to sell my latest product—me!

I began methodically executing my modified strategic planning approach. As a result, I was offered a position that required me to lead an organization approximately twice the size of my previous company. And I realized a 25 percent increase in my compensation package!

The purpose of this book is to arm you with a set of tools for methodically reestablishing your employment. These tools are what I used to obtain the position described in the previous paragraph. Of course, this is not a guarantee that you will get employed. However, my method will place you out in front of your unemployed colleagues and significantly increase your probability of success. I am writing this from a position of experience both in being laid off and in coaching people who need to reestablish their membership in the ranks of the employed. Like me, my coaching clients who have used these techniques have obtained positions far beyond their expectations. I am looking forward to coaching you as well.

Introduction

I Am Unemployed ... Now What Do I Do?: An Organized Approach to Becoming Employed will add power to your job search and ultimately your career. Finding books about how to get a job is easy. But finding a book that describes how to improve your main asset (*you*) has been hard ... until now.

First things first: *don't panic*. If you have read the preface, you know that you are not alone. You have taken the first step to executing a successful plan—you are reading this book.

You must realize that the job search process in itself is a full-time job. Be prepared to spend a great deal of time on this endeavor. Success requires focus, dedication, organization, preparation, effective goal setting, and a solid action plan. You should expect great rewards and compensation for doing this job well. However, as you will see when you review the Self-Marketing Plan Checklist, it is imperative that you also allocate free time on a daily basis. You need to spend time away from your job-search activities, just like you spend time away from work. This will help you to clear your mind, increase your creativity, and recharge your internal batteries. It will also help you to maintain focus.

Landing on the moon was not a one-step event. It took hundreds of thousands of steps to make that happen. The building of the international space station, with all of its living modules and test labs, was not a one-step event. It took millions of steps to create the space masterpiece that exists today. Finding a job is also *not* a one-step event. Fortunately, it won't take millions of steps. It will take just a few, laser-focused steps to fulfill your objective.

This book will help you to learn an effective job searching process *and* learn about yourself as well. You will be asked to understand your personal values; perform an assessment of your strengths, weaknesses, and skills; and assess the environment around you. This will be the foundation on which you build an efficient job search. It is absolutely imperative that you do not skip this step. It will be difficult for a potential employer to know you if you don't know yourself. In addition, it will help you to build the confidence necessary to land the job that suits your skills. The net result will be a successful *career* move versus simply landing a job. I currently have a coaching client who did not originally do a self-assessment. He consistently had trouble answering the interview question, "Could you tell me something about yourself?" He was able to answer that question *with ease*—his word, not mine— after completing the self-assessment.

Every business knows that merely having good products isn't enough. They need to be able to sell those products to the appropriate target audience. When a manufacturer wants you to buy their products, they develop an effective, targeted commercial message. They create a message that entices you to buy their product. Similarly, you are trying to sell your principal product—*you!* Therefore, this book will walk you through developing a commercial message to sell your product to prospective employers. In addition, you will be taught the steps to create the environment where you can deliver *your* commercial message.

The majority of available positions are not visible to the job seeker. Approximately, two-thirds of the available positions are in what is known as the *hidden* job market. These jobs are not advertised. This simply means they will not show up in employment agency files, online job websites, newspaper want ads, or company job postings. This is because, in some cases, they don't exist yet. Many of these jobs are replacement positions within a company. These jobs are filled in a variety of ways. Some are filled through internal *employee referral programs*. These are programs that reward employees for helping the company to find the right people for these jobs. The idea is that good employees know and will attract other good employees like them. In the long run, this approach also saves the company a great deal of money over using recruiting companies. This method is generally more effective in finding the *right* employee as well.

In many cases, jobs in the hidden market are filled by candidates who send unsolicited resumes to the company. The company matches the skills in these unsolicited resumes with the required skills in the open positions. They contact the candidates whose skills are most aligned with these positions. The public is generally never aware these positions ever existed!

The purpose of an effective cover letter and resume is to get an interview. Your purpose in the interview is to get hired into the position. It is also where you gain in-depth knowledge about the company, the interviewer, and the position. The company's objective is to learn as much as possible about you. Interviewers learn about your maturity level, attitude, enthusiasm, energy level, personality, sincerity, knowledge, and other important traits. Their objective is to ensure that there is a fit between you, the company, and the position. The question is, "How can you help them to satisfy that objective?" This book will teach you how to *control* the interview, by helping you to learn *interview mechanics*. Understanding interview mechanics makes you aware of questions you will be asked; helps you to determine which questions you should ask; and teaches you how to provide answers that will convince the interviewer that *you* are the one they should hire!

The techniques you will learn in this book will help you to identify and act on the positions that exist in both the visible and hidden job markets. In addition, it will provide you with the tools necessary to obtain those positions. Remember, even when there is 10 percent unemployment, someone is always looking for good people.

Are you ready to be hired?

How to Use This Book

To be successful you must commit to doing something every single day toward obtaining new employment. You will develop a strategy and a detailed plan as a result of following the action items in this book. You must either accomplish a step in your plan or an action item in this book. It doesn't matter which—just do something.

The *do something* directive is important because it is extremely easy to get paralyzed based on your current situation. You can get inundated and subsequently consumed by the bad news from the media, the negative thoughts of others, or just the shock of finding yourself in this position. You need to shake all of that off and get into action! This action-oriented approach will be the characteristic that helps you succeed while others continue in their current unemployed situations.

Now that you have committed to be an action-oriented person, let's get started.

I have organized this book into discreet sections. This means that you can go directly to the section that can help you at any point in your job search. For example, you may have already begun performing your job search before purchasing this book and a prospective employer has scheduled you for an interview. You can jump directly to the chapter entitled "Mastering the Interview." Everything that you need is contained within that chapter. In using this approach, some of the topics, ideas, techniques, and advice may be duplicated. I did this so that each chapter would contain all of the information that you need. Therefore, someone reading the book from beginning to end will begin to see some material that may appear similar to what was previously covered. You may choose to skip that material or reread it to solidify your understanding of the topic.

The best way to use this book is to proceed step by step through the chapters and complete the steps and then finally the tasks. This action approach has been laid out in an organized and logical fashion.

Many people have trouble reestablishing their employment because their approach to looking for a new job is like a shotgun blast—that is, all over the place. We need to make your approach more like a rifle shot: directed toward a specific target with extreme accuracy. This approach may not guarantee that you will quickly find a job. However, it will significantly increase your probability of success.

First read the quote for the particular task item before you. These are words of wisdom from some of the most influential people on the planet. You will see that many of these quotes have withstood the test of time. Next, read the section that describes the topic. This will give you a brief description of why these steps are important. It will also outline any preparation work that you should do before you begin the task. It is there to help you to quickly accomplish the tasks under "Action Steps for You." Begin doing the tasks listed in the "Action Steps for You" section. You may accomplish all of the tasks, or you may not. It is inevitable that you will learn some things that you didn't know that will need to be reviewed, investigated, or learned. You need to document these things in the "Additional Action Steps for You to Consider" section.

Devote time to an enjoyable pastime after completing your tasks for the day. This could be working on your hobby, playing with the kids, watching your favorite TV program, or engaging in any other activity that you enjoy. It is a requirement that you perform a favorite activity every day of your campaign. If you don't, you will spend your idle time worrying about where you are, an attitude that is not conducive to a successful job search and that can undo all that you have accomplished. Besides, you deserve a little playtime … You earned it.

At times, you may find that you are feeling like things are not working. If so, jump to the Improving Your Strategy Phase and assess the parts of your plan that may need some adjustments. Proceed with your plan once your assessment and subsequent adjustments to your plan are complete. The best way for you to quickly become successful is to get started … right now!

There is no such thing as saturation in education.

—Thomas Watson

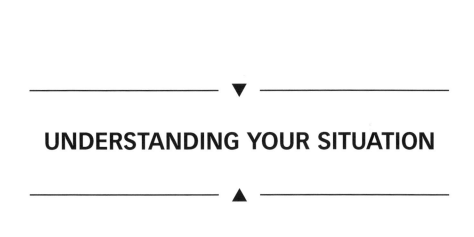

UNDERSTANDING YOUR SITUATION

Overview: Getting Organized

The primary objective of your job pursuit is to obtain permanent employment. There are many factors that can help or hinder your efforts to fulfill that objective. Therefore, it is extremely important that you have a detailed understanding of those factors.

The objective of this chapter is to help you take inventory of yourself and your current situation. The results of this inventory will be used later to develop your strategy and plans. It is important that you engage your family in this effort. They can be an excellent support base. In addition, they are directly impacted by the decisions you make.

This chapter will help you to look at all aspects of yourself. You will take an inventory of your own skills and abilities. Many job seekers bypass this step when pursuing new employment. Some items in your personal inventory may be a tremendous help or a significant impediment in achieving your goals, but you may be totally unaware of this fact. This chapter is designed to make you conscious of these items in your inventory. Later chapters in this book will show you how to enhance your strengths and either improve on or downplay your weaknesses.

Successful companies understand the things that can get in the way of their success. They perform a detailed analysis of themselves to identify those things internally. They also look at the external forces that can impact their ability to achieve their goals. They look at the internal strengths and weaknesses of the company. In addition, they analyze the opportunities that exist in the marketplace as well as the things that threaten their success. This is known as a SWOT analysis because it evaluates strengths, weaknesses, opportunities, and threats.

One of the primary objectives of this chapter is to help you to perform a personal SWOT analysis. You must be able to highlight your strengths to a potential employer. You can develop a plan to either strengthen or eliminate your weak areas. You can understand and learn to exploit those opportunities that may exist in the job market. Finally, you can develop a strategy to manage or eradicate the potential threats to the successful achievement of your goal. Later chapters in this book will show you how to enhance your strengths and either improve on or downplay your weaknesses.

It is extremely important that you fit in well with your new employer. That will be very difficult to do if you don't have a good understanding of yourself. This chapter will help you to develop that understanding.

Each of us knows and is connected to a large number of people. Every person you know, every person they know, and every person with whom you come into contact can be a potential resource in your job search effort. This chapter will assist you in identifying those resources. The success of your job search can be significantly improved when you learn to take advantage of the resources available to you.

Step 1
Assess Your Situation
Task 1: Engage Your Family

The family is one of nature's masterpieces.

—George Santayana

Involving Family

The first assessment that must be made is how your family is feeling about your current situation. It is important that they understand and work with you to accomplish your goal. You must involve the entire family in all aspects of your pursuit even if it is only by providing them status updates regarding your progress. It will be both uncomfortable and embarrassing for your family members to find things out from other sources. I gave these instructions to one of my corporate executive clients. To his surprise, he received a number of job leads from family members. Your family is your team and consists of your strongest allies. Use them.

Action Steps for You:

1. Hold a family meeting to inform all family members of your status.
2. Solicit your family's ideas on things that can be done.
3. Solicit your family's help and support as you proceed with your plans.
4. Schedule regular meetings designed to keep your family informed.
5. Record all additional family ideas in the space below.

Additional Action Steps for You to Consider:

1. _____
   _____
2. _____
   _____
3. _____
   _____
4. _____
   _____
5. _____
   _____

Step 1
Assess Your Situation
Task 2: Examine Your Finances

*A big part of financial freedom is having your heart
and mind free from worry about the what-ifs of life.*

—Suze Orman

Reviewing Your Finances

Based on your current situation, how long can you meet your short-term obligations without a steady income? It is important that you assess your current financial position. You must be able to determine the amount of time (based on your current financial position) that you can manage without a steady inflow of cash. You need to determine if you have the ability to meet your short-term obligations. A successful job search can sometimes take up to eighteen months.

Action Steps for You:

1. Prioritize your financial obligations by listing the most critical items first.
2. Determine how much is needed for rent or mortgage payments.
3. Create a detailed budget of your necessities (groceries, utilities, etc.).
4. Create a detailed budget for non–credit card obligations.
5. Create a detailed budget for credit card payments.
6. Determine the amount needed for monthly obligations based on the above.
7. Determine the number of months you can handle these obligations.

Additional Action Steps for You to Consider:

1. _____

2. _____

3. _____

4. _____

5. _____

Step 1
Assess Your Situation
Task 3: Your Home

You leave home to seek your fortune and, when you get it, you go home and share it with your family.

—Anita Baker

Keeping Your Home

One of the scariest aspects of being unemployed is the fear of losing your home. Make sure you understand what you need to do to keep this from happening. This is extremely important to both you and your family. Inform your lender of your situation if things get tight. They may be able to adjust your payments until you are employed again. I have learned that many lenders are willing to work with people once they are aware of the situation.

Action Steps for You:

1. Review the budget details from task two.
2. Determine the portion of your budget that is related to housing payments.
3. Ensure that the housing payment is the first amount allocated and paid.
4. Be prepared to contact your lender and discuss your situation.

Additional Action Steps for You to Consider:

1. _____
   _____
2. _____
   _____
3. _____
   _____
4. _____
   _____
5. _____
   _____

Step 1
Assess Your Situation
Task 4: Your Transportation

Car designers are just going to have to come up with an automobile that outlasts the payments.

—Erma Bombeck

Getting to Your Interviews

Assess your current transportation system. While many companies perform initial interviews by phone, most require subsequent interviews in person. Do you have adequate transportation for your job search? You must ensure that you have the ability to get to an interview when the opportunity becomes available. In addition, punctuality is extremely important. Make sure you allow enough time to arrive at your interview location.

Action Steps for You:

1. Assess the status of your current transportation.
2. Determine if your automobile(s) are operational.
3. Ensure that you have transportation to get to important appointments.
4. Study the bus and train schedules if that is your mode of travel.
5. Familiarize yourself with travel times between key locations.

Additional Action Steps for You to Consider:

1. _____
   _____
2. _____
   _____
3. _____
   _____
4. _____
   _____
5. _____
   _____

Step 2
Assess Yourself
Task 1: Your Focus

The secret of success is constancy of purpose.

—Benjamin Disraeli

Focusing on Goals

You must develop a habit of being focused on your goal. There will be a number of things that will distract you from your primary objective. This includes your attitude, which can be the biggest obstacle to your progress. You may feel like your current situation is your fault. It has been my experience in dealing with many people that this is not true. You must develop a constancy of purpose and the ability to focus on getting things accomplished. Be aware of those things that can deter you from making daily progress and eliminate them. I got distracted the first time I was laid off. I focused on catching up on my house chores and hobbies instead of looking for work. I regained my focus once I realized that two months had gone by without any progress being made on my job search.

Action Steps for You:

1. List the tasks that you do that will not help you reach your goal.
2. List the tasks that others give you that will not help your progress.
3. Determine which of those unhelpful tasks are essential to do anyway.
4. Allocate time outside the workweek to complete the unhelpful tasks.
5. Check off nonessential tasks as you complete them.
6. Maintain a positive attitude.

Additional Action Steps for You to Consider:

1. _____
   _____
2. _____
   _____
3. _____
   _____
4. _____
   _____
5. _____
   _____

Step 2
Assess Yourself
Task 2: Your Strengths

Character is doing the right thing when no one is watching.

—Unknown

Knowing Your Strengths

It's important to know the skills and character attributes that make you a valuable person to prospective employers. You should take some time to make sure that you understand all aspects of your strengths. Review the self-assessment process detailed on pages 16–22. I have found that this process has been helpful to all of my clients.

Action Steps for You:

1. List the positive aspects of your character such as honesty, integrity, and so on.
2. Write down your key skills and abilities.
3. Ask family members, friends, and former coworkers to assess your strengths.
4. Complete the self-assessment forms on the following pages.

Additional Action Steps for You to Consider:

1. _____
   _____

2. _____
   _____

3. _____
   _____

4. _____
   _____

5. _____
   _____

Self-Assessment Forms

Personal Skills Assessment

SKILLS ASSESSMENT

MY NAME   TODAY'S DATE

SKILL	1	2	3	4	5	NOTES / COMMENTS

Figure 1: Personal Skills Assessment Sheet

Instructions for Your Personal Skills Assessment

Take a sheet of paper and write "Skills Assessment" at the top of the page (see Figure 1: Personal Skills Assessment Sheet). Write your name and the current date below the title. Segment the page into seven columns. Label the first column "Skill." Make sure it is a wide column. This is where you will list the skills that you have. Make the next five columns small and number them one through five. This is where you will rate your skill level. Remember, this is *your* sheet. No one else is going to see the skills or your ratings unless you show the form to them. (Later, I will define what each rating represents.) Finally, label the last column, "Notes/Comments." This is where you will make any notes or comments to yourself on skills that you rate a one or five.

Now you are ready to begin. The first step is to list as many of your skills as possible on the sheet. You should do this over a five- to seven-day period. The reason is that, as time passes, you will remember more and more of your skills that you might not use on a regular basis. It is natural for you to initially list all of the skills that you use regularly; however, if you are like most people, those are not all of the skills you have. Thus, you should keep this sheet with you and add skills in the skills column as you think of them.

Next, you will rate each of your skills on a scale of one to five once you are comfortable that you have listed *all* of your skills. Don't get too concerned if you think of more skills during this phase. Simply, add the new skills to the bottom of the skills column. Feel free to add sheets of paper if all of your skills cannot fit on one sheet. When you are ready, rate each skill using the definitions below.

Ratings for Your Personal Skills Assessment

- **1**–Use this rating if you essentially have very little expertise or very old knowledge in this skill. You should also use this rating if you have significant expertise in this area but have not used it in a really long time. Remember to make a special note or comment to yourself about this rating. For example, you may write, "My future plans don't depend on me having this skill," or "I really need to increase my expertise in this skill."

17

- **2**–Use this rating if you have expertise in this area but could use more knowledge, education, or experience in order to increase your skill level to average.
- **3**–Use this rating when your skill level, knowledge, or expertise is average.
- **4**–Use this rating when your knowledge, skill level, or expertise is above average, but you would need some additional experience or education in order to be considered an expert in this area.
- **5**–Use this rating if you are clearly recognized as an expert in this area. Your knowledge, expertise, education, or skill level is clearly superior to that of most people. You may be (or may have been) publically recognized as having advanced expertise in this area. Remember to make a special note or comment to yourself about this rating. For example, "Increase other people's awareness that I have this skill," or "My future plans don't require this expertise."

Place the sheet(s) in a folder when you think you have captured all of the items.

Personal Likes and Dislikes

LIKES AND DISLIKES

MY NAME   TODAY'S DATE

LIKES	DISLIKES

Figure 2: Likes-and-Dislikes Sheet

Instructions for Your Personal Likes-and-Dislikes Assessment

Document your likes and dislikes. Take a sheet of paper and title it "Likes and Dislikes" (see Figure 2: Likes-and-Dislikes Sheet). Put your name and the current date on the top of the sheet. Create two columns on the sheet. Label one column "Likes," and label the other column "Dislikes."

Begin listing the things you really like doing. These could be things that you do in your professional career or things you do that as part of a hobby or your social or charitable activities. As you can see, it doesn't matter where or when you do these things—but simply, that you like doing them. You should make this list over a three- to five- day period. Keep this sheet near you and add items as you think of them.

Do the exact same thing with the "Dislikes" side of the column. These will be activities that you really dislike doing. Don't be concerned with the *degree* to which you dislike doing these activities. It is simply important to know that you dislike doing them.

Some people prefer to place their dislikes on the back of the page so that it is not visible when they are listing their likes and vice versa. Either way is fine. It is just important to list as many of these activities as you can.

Place the sheet in a folder when you think you have exhausted your list of likes and dislikes.

Do WELL /DON'T DO WELL

MY NAME   TODAY'S DATE

I DO WELL	I DON'T DO SO WELL

Figure 3: Do-Well and Don't-Do-So-Well Sheet

Instructions for Your Personal Do-Well and Don't-Do-So-Well Assessment

You are now ready to inventory those things that you are really good at doing and those things that you are not so good at doing.

Take a sheet of paper and place "Do Well/Don't Do So Well" at the top of the page (see Figure 3: Do-Well and Don't-Do-So-Well Sheet). Put your name and the current date at the top of the page. Create two columns. Label one column "I Do Well" and the other "I Don't Do So Well." Some people like to place the "I Don't Do So Well" list on the back side of the sheet. Either way is fine.

Think of all of the things that you do: big tasks, little tasks, complex tasks, and simple tasks. The size of the tasks and details about when and where you perform them are not important. It is more important that you capture the things that you do and don't do well. Fill this out over a three- to five-day period, adding items as you think of them.

Repeat the process for those items that you don't do well.

Place the sheet(s) in a folder when you think you have captured all of the items.

Step 2
Assess Yourself
Task 3: Your Weaknesses

There are only two ways to live your life.
One is as though nothing is a miracle.
The other is as though everything is a miracle.

—Albert Einstein

Knowing Your Weaknesses

Your mere existence is a miracle. However, you may not feel that way when you consider your weak points. Like your strengths, your weaknesses are a part of who you are and you need to understand them. Knowing your weaknesses will help you to determine how to eliminate or minimize them. Hiding them is not an option. For example, one of your weaknesses could be procrastination. You may not work right away on assignments that are given to you. You should practice doing things as soon as you are asked to do them. Another weakness could be time management. You may easily get distracted by nonessential tasks. Your solution might be to practice making a to-do list each day. Place the items on the list in order of importance and check off each item as you complete it.

Action Steps for You:

1. List those items that you think are your weaknesses.
2. Ask family members, friends, and former coworkers to assess your weaknesses.
3. Determine which items on the list will interfere with obtaining your goal.
4. Develop a plan to eliminate or improve the items identified in step three above.

Additional Action Steps for You to Consider:

1. _____
   _____
2. _____
   _____
3. _____
   _____
4. _____
   _____
5. _____
   _____

Step 2
Assess Yourself
Task 4: Your Opportunities

*It is better to be prepared for an opportunity and not have
one than to have an opportunity and not be prepared.*

—Whitney M. Young Jr.

Seeing Opportunities

Opportunity exists everywhere. Sometimes it exists in your strengths,
sometimes in your weaknesses. For example, you may think that being
a very detail-oriented, "fussy" person is a weakness. However, there are
many positions, in systems analysis for example, in which that would be
considered a strong point. Job opportunities may exist with things that
are occurring in your neighborhood or in your local coffee shop. Many
executives routinely start their days in local coffee shops. They access
their e-mails while drinking their morning coffee. You must look and
listen for potential opportunities that could help you obtain your goal.
You may lose the chance to pursue a job simply by not looking for the
opportunities that are around you.

Action Steps for You:

1. Think of places where you can see or hear of opportunities.
2. List the names of people who can keep you abreast of important
   news.
3. Consider all sources of information that could provide signs of
   opportunities.
4. Obtain publications that you can read to look for opportunities.
5. Allocate time to pursue those people, places, and things you listed
   above.

Additional Action Steps for You to Consider:

1. _____
   _____
2. _____
   _____
3. _____
   _____
4. _____
   _____
5. _____
   _____

Step 2
Assess Yourself
Task 5: Your Threats

Your objective, as a job seeker, is to create the future vision for your family that is filled with hope, excitement, and success.

—Wayne L. Anderson

Job Search Obstacles

Threats are those things that will get in the way of you obtaining your goal, be they other people, unproductive tasks, meaningless distractions, or simply procrastination and bad habits. For example, when people know that you are available during the day, they may ask for your help on various things. I was constantly asked to help other volunteers with events around town. Spending time on those events would have impacted my ability to complete my job search. I promised to participate after I found a job. Keep in mind that your objective is to create a positive future for yourself and your family; therefore, you must understand and eliminate those things that threaten your ability to be successful. Allocate time *outside of your prime time* to perform those distracting items that are essential for you to complete.

Action Steps for You:

1. List habits of yours that could get in the way of attaining your goal.
2. Determine the unproductive tasks that consistently block your progress.
3. List people who unnecessarily take up your productive time.
4. Determine those distractions that it is essential to complete at some time.
5. Allocate nonprime time to eliminate those threats to your success.

Additional Action Steps for You to Consider:

1. _____
_____

2. _____
_____

3. _____
_____

4. _____
_____

5. _____
_____

Step 3
Assess Your Market
Task 1: Your Market Value

We get paid for bringing value to the marketplace.

—Jim Rohn

Knowing Your Market Value

You increase your probability of being considered by a prospective company when you understand the types of companies where you can bring value. For example, you may be good with numbers and figures, which means you can provide value to companies that are in industries that provide accounting or bookkeeping services. You need to determine the industries that have the most use for your services. You can go to your local library to find references that will tell you which companies are in those industries. Then call the human-resources departments in those companies to determine their hiring status. Send them your resume.

Action Steps for You:

1. List the industries that can best use your skills.
2. Determine which companies are in those industries.
3. Select companies that are in your relocation or commute areas.
4. Review publications and online sources for companies that are hiring.
5. Get help finding contact information at local libraries.
6. Contact the companies' human-resources departments and ask if they are hiring.
7. Indentify primary, secondary, and tertiary companies to target your plan.

Additional Action Steps for You to Consider:

1. _____
   _____

2. _____
   _____

3. _____
   _____

4. _____
   _____

5. _____
   _____

Step 3
Assess Your Market
Task 2: Your Distant Market Location

*Demand is not slowing down. It's just
going to another location.*

—David Lereah

Knowing Where Jobs Are

There are companies all over that are growing and hiring people to help them grow. Some will be local and some will not. It is important for you to determine your tolerance for going outside of your current geographical location in order to become employed. This does not always mean that you must completely move yourself and your family; however, it may mean that you have to develop a longer commute than normal to fulfill your goal. I have a client who accepted a job that required an hour-and–a-half commute, but the job was a perfect match for his skills and provided excellent compensation.

Action Steps for You:

1. List the companies outside your area that are in your designated industries.
2. Identify the companies on the list that are hiring.
3. Determine if you are flexible about leaving your current location.
4. Determine which companies can best utilize your skills.
5. Decide how far you are willing to travel to obtain employment.

Additional Action Steps for You to Consider:

1. _____
_____

2. _____
_____

3. _____
_____

4. _____
_____

5. _____
_____

Step 3
Assess Your Market
Task 3: Your Market Contacts

It is only when I lose contact with the painting that the result is a mess. Otherwise there is pure harmony, an easy give and take, and the painting comes out well.

—Jackson Pollock

Staying in Contact

You need to keep in contact with people you know in those industries that can use your skills. It is always important that you maintain connections in your target industries. For example, one of my clients was targeting employment in the information technology industry. She did not realize initially the number of friends she had in that industry who were willing to help her with her job search. We will discuss this topic more when we talk about building your network.

Action Steps for You:

1. Review the industries that can use your talents and skills.
2. Determine which companies you want to target.
3. Select the companies at which you may have contacts.
4. Make a list of everyone you know who has worked for any of these companies.
5. File the list of people and companies for use when developing your network.

Additional Action Steps for You to Consider:

1. _____
   _____

2. _____
   _____

3. _____
   _____

4. _____
   _____

5. _____
   _____

Step 3
Assess Your Market
Task 4: Markets You Should Avoid

There is nothing quite so useless, as doing with great efficiency, something that should not be done at all.

—Peter F. Drucker

The Right Markets

It is easy to target all companies in all industries when performing a job search. This may be a good approach if you have a skill that can be used anywhere in any company. However, if your skills are specialized to a particular industry or set of industries, you could be wasting a great deal of time and energy with no results. You need to focus your energies on those industries and companies that will yield the highest probability of success in your search. For example, if you are in the information technology field, most companies with more than one hundred employees can use your skills. However, I have a client who is a biochemical engineer. The types of companies that can use her skills are limited. Therefore, she had to narrow the industries and companies in which she targeted her search.

Action Steps for You:

1. Review your list of industries.
2. Review your list of local and distant companies.
3. Review those companies that will benefit from your skills.
4. File the listing of industries and companies in the event your strategy changes.

Additional Action Steps for You to Consider:

1. _____

2. _____

3. _____

4. _____

5. _____

Step 4
Assess Your Network
Task 1: Networking Tools

Do not go where the path may lead, go instead
where there is no path and leave a trail.

—Ralph Waldo Emerson

Networking Techniques

Is a fear of new technology keeping you from establishing an online presence? Or are you just not familiar with online social media techniques? Many people are searching for jobs online. These people generally just look at the job sites of particular companies. This is a good approach to begin with; however, there are a number of other online sources that are sometimes ignored that can be just as effective—if not more effective. For example, many employers review the LinkedIn or Facebook profiles of people with resumes in which they have an interest. A complete profile is like a mini-resume online. You can include details about your past positions, schools that you have attended, and your accomplishments. In addition, a very powerful feature of LinkedIn is that you can have friends, acquaintances, former coworkers, and former employers write recommendations for you. Your prospective employer will read these like references.

You must ensure that your online profile is written well. Make sure that there are no misspellings or grammatical errors. This can impact how your prospective employer may view your work. In addition, make certain that the information in your profile is extremely accurate. It is becoming common for employers to research this information before calling people in for interviews.

I have personally received management consulting contracts, coaching contracts, and job offers solely based on my LinkedIn profile.

You should explore the vast amount of online information that is available to you, including job listings. Look for the required skills identified in the listings. Adjust your online profile to display the skills of yours that match the skills employers need.

Action Steps for You:

1. Search and list recruiting companies that specialize in your skills.
2. Create a profile on LinkedIn that highlights your skills.
3. Find and create a profile on other social-networking sites like Facebook.
4. Search and list job sites where you can discover hiring companies.
5. Find blogs or chat sites that specialize in your area of expertise.

Additional Action Steps for You to Consider:

1. _____
   _____
2. _____
   _____
3. _____
   _____
4. _____
   _____
5. _____
   _____

Step 4
Assess Your Network
Task 2: Your Colleagues

*Great discoveries and achievements invariably
involve the cooperation of many minds.*

—Alexander Graham Bell

Networking with Former Coworkers

You came into contact with a number of people when you were
employed. Some of the people were colleagues you worked with in
your department or other departments. Some were salespeople who
were selling products to you on a regular basis. Others may have been
professionals who repaired your equipment. All are resources who can
help you to achieve your goals. You need to use as many minds as are
available to you to help you reach your goal. For example, a salesperson
who sells products to you usually sells to other companies in the same
industry. Many people talk to salespeople about things that are going
on in their companies—including positions that they are trying to
fill—so these contacts may know of job openings at companies in your
industry.

Action Steps for You:

1. List the positions you held in the past ten years.
2. List the people you came into contact with in each position you
   held.
3. Search online networks for companies with which you did
   business.
4. Search for people in those companies with whom you had contact.
5. Call or send notes or e-mails to set meetings with the people on
   your list.

Additional Action Steps for You to Consider:

1. _____
   _____
2. _____
   _____
3. _____
   _____
4. _____
   _____
5. _____
   _____

Step 4
Assess Your Network
Task 3: Your Friends

*"If you go looking for a friend,
you're going to find they're very scarce.
If you go out to be a friend,
you'll find them everywhere."*

—Zig Ziglar

Talking with Friends

You have many friends. You have been a friend to many. Your friends will be willing to help you be successful just as you would help them if they needed you. It is important that you think of all the friends you have developed over the years. Be careful not to judge whether or not *you think* they can be of assistance to you. It is imperative that you let them make that decision.

I made friends with the janitor of a company I worked for merely by saying hello to him each morning when I arrived. A number of years later, that janitor helped me to acquire a senior position in the company. I was not aware that when I saw him as a janitor, he was actually working his way through school, earning a master's degree in finance. He was the head of the finance department when he helped me with my career.

A coaching client related a story to me about how he was contacted by a high school friend. His friend got in touch with him after seeing his profile on the LinkedIn website. My client was able to help his friend to secure first a consulting position and later a full-time position in the company where he was employed. He had not seen or heard from his high school friend in almost fifteen years!

Action Steps for You:

1. List every friend that immediately comes to mind.
2. Make a list of additional friends and acquaintances that you know.
3. Search online networks for friends that you have not seen for a while.
4. Search for other people with whom you once had contact.
5. Perform these steps multiple times until you have a complete list.

Additional Action Steps for You to Consider:

1. _____
   _____
2. _____
   _____
3. _____
   _____
4. _____
   _____
5. _____
   _____

Step 4
Assess Your Network
Task 4: Your Family

*After all, when you come right down to it, how
many people speak the same language even
when they speak the same language?*

—Russell Hoban

Help from Family Members

It is easy, for some, to feel like other people in their family don't speak the same language they do. It is also easy to dismiss the help of family members, for whatever reasons, but you must pursue the help of family members just as you would people who are not in your family. They are not only the people closest to you but are also generally the ones who will put the most effort into helping you succeed. Be careful not to judge whether or not *you think* they can be of assistance to you—just let them help.

At one point, my brother, Terry, was looking for a better position. I was well aware that I could not help him in the industry where he was seeking work. But I am an adjunct professor in business and management, and I teach a course in business communications; therefore, I was able to help him by reviewing his resume, cover letters, and e-mail messages. I helped him to deliver the key messages in each of his communication channels.

There are a number of ways in which your family can help you, sometimes directly, sometimes indirectly.

Action Steps for You:

1. List all of your immediate family members.
2. List family members that can be easily contacted.
3. Search online networks for family that you have not seen for a while.
4. Search for other family members with whom you have lost contact.
5. Perform these steps multiple times until you have a complete list.

Additional Action Steps for You to Consider:

1. _____
   _____
2. _____
   _____
3. _____
   _____
4. _____
   _____
5. _____
   _____

Step 4
Assess Your Network
Task 5: Your Past Employers

You have not converted a man because you have silenced him.

— John Morley

Contacting Past Employers

As you read in the preface, being laid off, in most cases, has nothing to do with your level of performance. In addition, contrary to popular belief, the manager who laid you off probably feels extremely bad that he or she had to execute such an action, so that same person can be your biggest ally when you are trying to secure a new position. Managers obviously cannot silence you just by laying you off. You need to use them as *personal* contacts rather than leveraging their position in the company since they may be limited in how much they can say as representatives of the company.

You should avoid previous employers with whom you did not have a good relationship. You can find this out from them in your initial contact. I once left a company for a better position in another company. I'd had an excellent relationship with my boss, who was the vice president of the department, so I naturally felt comfortable using him as a reference. He did not give me a bad reference—he simply told the executive recruiter that he didn't know me! I did not realize that he was terribly upset that I was leaving the company. I called him, and we had a brief meeting over coffee. He subsequently called the executive recruiter and gave me a glowing review. This was not a layoff situation, but it clearly highlights the importance of knowing how your previous employer thinks about you before using them to help with your search.

A good contact would be a previous supervisor who indicated that he or she really enjoyed working with you and/or hated to see you leave. A previous employer may have clearly stated that your performance had nothing to do with your being laid off. They may be willing to write you a letter of reference. In addition, they may be open to writing a referral for you on your online social media profile. This could be a very effective contact.

Action Steps for You:

1. List the previous companies in which you have worked.
2. List the people within those companies to whom you directly reported.
3. Select people to whom you did not directly report but who are good contacts.
4. Identify the people with whom you had the best relationships.
5. Categorize the rest as secondary contacts.

Additional Action Steps for You to Consider:

1. _____

2. _____

3. _____

4. _____

5. _____

DEVELOPING YOUR STRATEGY

Overview:
Creating Your Job-search strategy

One of my favorite childhood stories is *Alice in Wonderland* because there are so many things it can teach us.

In one part of the story, Alice is on a road with which she was not familiar. She arrives at a fork in the road after leaving the duchess's house and meets the Cheshire cat in a tree. The cat constantly grins. It can disappear and reappear whenever it likes. Sometimes the cat disappears and, amazingly enough, leaves its grin behind. Alice and the Cheshire cat have an exchange that goes like this:

"Cheshire Puss," [Alice] began, rather timidly, as she did not at all know whether it would like the name: however, it only grinned a little wider. Alice went on, "Would you tell me, please, which way I ought to go from here?"

"That depends a good deal on where you want to get to," said the Cat.

"I don't much care where—" said Alice.

"Then it doesn't matter which way you go," said the Cat.

"—so long as I get SOMEWHERE," Alice added as an explanation.

"Oh, you're sure to do that," said the Cat, "if you only walk long enough."

This conversation teaches us that if we don't know where we want to go, then any road will get us there!

It is not unusual for a job seeker to aimlessly pursue employment without knowing where he is going. In essence, the person doesn't have a plan. The objective of this section is to help you to understand where you want to go with *your* job search. I will assist you in developing a strategy for approaching your job search. I will teach you how to plan, if you are not familiar with planning techniques. You will learn to develop all aspects of your plan, from analyzing the skills that are needed in the marketplace to setting daily goals for yourself. Finally, I will show you techniques for testing your plan to ensure that it will work—before you begin using it.

I am always amazed at how much time people will spend planning their vacations as compared to their job searches. They can tell you, in great detail, everything they are going to do on each day of their vacations. However, those same people are baffled when asked how they plan to approach their job searches. In this chapter, I will help you to be very clear as to how you will approach each day of your job search endeavor. You will be astonished at how planning your activities will help you to stay on target and quickly attain your goal.

Step 1
Develop Your Strategy
Task 1: Your Vision

Always listen to experts. They'll tell you what can't be done and why. Then do it.

—Robert A. Heinlein

Having a Vision

Do you know what your ideal job or position looks like? Can you imagine yourself in that position?

The first step in developing any good strategy is creating a vision. This is a clear picture in your mind of your ideal position. It is a mental image of your ultimate job. This is the position that you dream about all the time. It is the position that tells you that you have reached the pinnacle of success. You may think of it as a *super* goal, a goal on steroids.

The following is the actual vision of one of my executive clients:

I am the vice president of XYZ Company with a large corner office on the seventeenth floor of the Times Building. I sit in a large leather chair behind a cherry-wood desk and direct the US and European operations.

There will be a large number of experts that will be available to explain what you should be doing and how to do it. They will be equally clear about what you can't do. It is imperative that you develop your own vision of success. You need to formulate a strategy that will fulfill your vision of what success means to you. Corporations develop visions of what success is for them. Sports celebrities develop visions of success in their respective endeavors. A clear vision will help direct your energy, focus your attention, and ensure your forward progress.

A personal vision statement communicates your ideal end result. Unlike a goal, a vision rarely changes. It is a reason for our existence. It guides you in the decisions you make and the directions you take. Your vision can be how you see yourself in a few months or a few years. See yourself as the person you want to be. It is a picture of your true self in the future. When developing your vision, you imagine what you are doing, who you are with, what you have accomplished, what is important to you, and how people are relating to you in the future. It is a statement of what success means to you and who you want to become.

Action Steps for You:

1.   Close your eyes and picture yourself in the future.
2.   Include all of the important elements of your life and career in the picture.
3.   Reflect on your vision of what success means to you.
4.   Determine whether success is just getting employed.
5.   Determine whether success is achieving a financial goal.
6.   Create an image of how you will feel in the future after achieving your success.
7.   Open your eyes and write down in detail what you saw when your eyes were closed.
8.   Write down a clear, detailed description of the ideal job that will help you create you new future.
9.   Think of where you are today and write the steps you need to take to get to your new future.

Additional Action Steps for You to Consider:

1.   _____

2.   _____

3.   _____

4.   _____

5.   _____

Step 1
Develop Your Strategy
Task 2: Your Mission

*Every person above the ordinary has a certain
mission that they are called to fulfill.*

—Johann Wolfgang von Goethe

Having a Mission

A mission is about who you are and why you do what you do. Even
more so it is about your purpose and values. Your vision helped you to
vividly imagine where you would like to be. Your mission establishes the
strategy to achieve that vision. Your mission may appear obvious: get a
job. But the next question is *Why do you want a job?* It may be to pay
bills, to take your family on a well-deserved trip, to upgrade your worn-
out wardrobe, or whatever other reason for which you are pursuing
employment. Regardless of the reasons, you need to be clear about
them, and they need to be written down. Your mission will provide a
reason for completing every step of your plan.

Action Steps for You:

1. List the three to five reasons why you are pursuing employment.
2. Describe the positive aspects of fulfilling each reason.
3. Write down the consequences of *not* fulfilling each reason.
4. Envision how you will feel once each reason is satisfied.
5. Describe how you will reward yourself once each reason is
    satisfied.

Additional Action Steps for You to Consider:

1. _____
   _____
2. _____
   _____
3. _____
   _____
4. _____
   _____
5. _____
   _____

Step 1
Develop Your Strategy
Task 3: Your Time-Management Strategy

You will never find time for anything. If
you want time, you must make it.

—Charles Bixton

Time Management

Progress toward successfully completing your plan can be seriously hindered due to poor time management. One of your worst enemies is procrastination. It is important that you schedule time for all of the things that are important to you. Those things include time for your job search, family, hobbies, building and maintaining relationships, and so on. This will ensure that you will complete the job-search actions that must be taken care of, as well as the other activities that are important to you.

Action Steps for You:

1. Determine the time each day that will be devoted to job-search activities.
2. Ensure that you have access to the tools and equipment you need to do these activities.
3. List the other activities that you do in a week that are important to you.
4. Determine which day each activity should be performed.
5. Determine and allocate the time for each activity unrelated to your job search.

Additional Action Steps for You to Consider:

1. _____
   _____

2. _____
   _____

3. _____
   _____

4. _____
   _____

5. _____
   _____

Step 1
Develop Your Strategy
Task 4: Your Financial Strategy

*I know at last what distinguishes man
from animals; financial worries.*

—Romain Rolland

Financial Strategy

You need to establish a budget that will help you to avoid financial worries. There may be some cost to performing a job search. You may need to travel to interviews, upgrade your wardrobe, purchase books and materials about interviewing and prospective companies, upgrade your computer, and so on. In addition to establishing your household budget, you will need to establish a job-search budget so that there are no financial surprises.

Action Steps for You:

1. List the costs that may be associated with your job-search campaign.
2. Determine the most appropriate time to spend these amounts.
3. Integrate these expenditures into your household budget.
4. Adjust your overall spending strategy to minimize financial worries.
5. Allocate time each week to review that status of your spending plan.

Additional Action Steps for You to Consider:

1. _____
   _____
2. _____
   _____
3. _____
   _____
4. _____
   _____
5. _____
   _____

Step 1
Develop Your Strategy
Task 5: First Impressions

There are four ways, and only four ways, in which we have contact with the world. We are evaluated and classified by these four contacts: what we do, how we look, what we say, and how we say it.

—Dale Carnegie

First Impressions

It is imperative that you engage your outside contacts only when you are ready. You can seriously (and negatively) impact your *first impression* when you begin contacting people in your network without a well-thought-out plan. This is especially true for people who may not know you well. You may be tempted to jump in and use the many online tools that are available to you. However, what you do, how you look, what you say, and how you say it in the online world could be the difference between success and failure in your job search endeavors. There are two ways to make a good first impression: one is in person, and the other is online.

You have about thirty seconds to make an impact when you meet someone in person. Their impression is developed from how you are dressed, how you walk, whom you were previously talking with, and the first words out of your mouth.

In an online environment, people can't see you. They can't see your facial expressions; they can't see your body language; and they can't hear your voice. Therefore, they concentrate on your writing style, the topics you write about, the pictures that you post (or that are posted of you), and, in a social media website, the people to whom you are connected.

Action Steps for You:

1. First Impressions in Person
    a. Make sure you are dressed appropriately for the occasion.
    b. Good grooming includes personal hygiene and cleanliness.
    c. A firm and confident handshake is basic to making a good first impression.
    d. Make sure you appear confident when introducing yourself.
    e. Start a conversation by asking an open-ended question and then be quiet and listen to the answer. This shows the person you are truly interested.
    f. Demonstrate good manners.
    g. Avoid being overly aggressive during the first meeting.
    h. Be courteous.

2. First Impressions Online
    a. Write down what you want to achieve by placing your information online.
    b. Write on a piece of paper what you plan to place online.
    c. Have a friend or family member read and comment on your writing. Make sure they check your grammar and spelling.
    d. Tell your friend or family member what you plan to achieve by placing the information online.
    e. Ask them about their first impressions of what you wrote.
    f. Make modifications that fit your objectives based on their suggestions.
    g. Have someone give you his or her opinion about any pictures that you plan to place online.

Additional Action Steps for You to Consider:

1. _____
   _____
2. _____
   _____
3. _____
   _____
4. _____
   _____
5. _____
   _____

Step 2
Plan for the Plan
Task 1: Your Goals

*If you don't know where you are going, you
will probably wind up someplace else.*

—Yogi Berra

Written Goals

Many job seekers spend more time preparing for family vacations than
they do planning for their careers. They move through their careers
without really knowing where they are going. The odds of being
successful in any endeavor significantly increase when a person has
written goals. Ninety-eight percent of successful people have written
goals. You should plan to join that elite group.

Action Steps for You:

1. Write down the goals you previously developed.
2. Write down your goals for the type of position you are pursuing.
3. Describe the ideal company that you want to hire you.
4. Document your financial goals for the next two to three years.
5. Document any additional personal goals that are important to
    you.

Additional Action Steps for You to Consider:

1. _____

2. _____

3. _____

4. _____

5. _____

Step 2
Plan for the Plan
Task 2: Reviewing Your Options

You may be disappointed if you fail, but
you are doomed if you don't try.

—Beverly Sills

Being an Independent Consultant

An option that is often overlooked when approaching a job search is the ability to market yourself as a consultant. You have accumulated a lot of knowledge and a great deal of skills over the years. As a result of the economy and downsizing, companies are turning to temporary help to get their work done. They no longer have the needed skills in-house. Many companies may not need your skills on a permanent basis but may be willing to "purchase" those skills for a period of time at a very lucrative price. This scenario is not restricted to any particular industry.

You could be hired as a consultant in your field to train other people in your area of expertise. A company might need someone with your skill set for technical advice. Early in my career I was skilled in the area of information technology. I consulted with companies on how to establish information technology strategies after I was laid off. There are a number of books, courses, and reference materials on how to establish yourself as an independent consultant. There are even consultants that will help you to become a consultant!

Action Steps for You:

1. Take out your list of skills.
2. Take out your list of the things that you do well.
3. Take out your list of the things you like to do.
4. Create a consulting resume using the functional-resume format.
5. Look for companies that may need your skills.
6. Acquire and study books and materials on how to become an independent consultant.

Additional Action Steps for You to Consider:

1. _____
   _____
2. _____
   _____
3. _____
   _____
4. _____
   _____
5. _____
   _____

Step 2
Plan for the Plan
Task 3: Prepare for Opportunities

Good fortune is what happens when
opportunity meets with planning.

—Thomas A. Edison

Taking Advantage of Opportunities

There are opportunities in every endeavor, but *planning* is what makes an opportunity a reality. There will be many opportunities as you embark on your job search. Many of them will not be intuitively obvious. In addition, they may not always be related to your job search.

Opportunities may surface when you are talking to your contacts. For example, your friend may mention the name of a company that is new to your area; new companies usually hire right away. Or you may read about something in the paper. An opportunity could present itself while you are having breakfast with an old colleague or may be a result of a number of events that occur over a few days. Once, soon after being laid off, I was having breakfast with a friend, and he told me about one of our former colleagues who had gotten promoted. I sent her a card congratulating her on her new promotion. She replied with a thank-you note and asked me how I was doing. After a few such exchanges and a trip from Maine to Texas, I was hired as a senior vice president—for a job that had not previously existed.

In any case, you won't see opportunities if you are not looking for them, and thus, you will not reap the fortunes that potential opportunities may contain.

Action Steps for You:

1. Create a page in your notebook entitled "Potential Opportunities."
2. Write opportunities down whenever they present themselves.
3. Be prepared to create a plan to pursue potential opportunities.
4. Allocate time just to reflect on events that have occurred and consider how they might prove to be opportunities.

Additional Action Steps for You to Consider:

1. _____
    _____
2. _____
    _____
3. _____
    _____
4. _____
    _____
5. _____
    _____

Step 2
Plan for the Plan
Task 4: Assessing Your Tools

The new information technology—Internet and e-mail—have practically eliminated the physical costs of communications.

—Peter Drucker

Using Electronic Tools

There are lots of different types of technology and equipment that you will need to help save time. You will need equipment such as computers, telephones, a copier, and so on. Some of the equipment you need you may have; some you may not have. It is imperative that you know what technology and equipment you will need, and you also need to determine how you will get access to the equipment you may not have. You will significantly increase your control over the success of your plan if you have all of the necessary technology available to you when you need it.

Action Steps for You:

1. Determine if you have the equipment needed to execute your plans.
2. Determine equipment that you need that you *don't* have (for example, a copier).
3. List resources that may have additional equipment, such as the public library.
4. List the various online sources that you will use.
5. Acquire access to equipment that you need and don't have.

Additional Action Steps for You to Consider:

1. _____

2. _____

3. _____

4. _____

5. _____

Step 2
Plan for the Plan
Task 5: Create Your Resume

*The closest to perfection a person ever comes is
when he fills out a job application form.*

—Stanley J. Randall

Creating a Resume

Later, when you begin executing your plan, you will identify different
job opportunities. Some may highlight one of your skills while others
may require different skills. Therefore, it may be necessary occasionally
to rearrange your resume. In other words, although your skills are the
same, you will present them differently depending on the requirements
of each position. In addition, there are multiple types of resume formats
(chronological, skill-based, narrative, and so on). You should have a least
one version of your resume in each format. Remember, they will contain
the same skills information, but it will just be presented differently.
There are numerous resources available both online and in books that
will help you develop an effective set of resumes.

Action Steps for You:

1. Take out your completed self-assessment forms.
2. Review the skills listed to ensure you have a complete list.
3. Take out your strengths, weaknesses, and threats.
4. Create a strong resume by highlighting your strengths using the
    information you collected about yourself.
5. Create different types of resumes (chronological, functional, etc.)
    using the same information.

Additional Action Steps for You to Consider:

1. _____

2. _____

3. _____

4. _____

5. _____

Step 3
Develop Your Plan
Task 1: Skills to Market

If you fail to plan, you plan to fail by default.

—Unknown

Identifying Marketable Skills

Many people will spend more time planning their vacations than planning how to reenter the workforce. You need to plan every aspect of your job-search campaign. For example, just knowing that you have a set of skills does not necessarily mean that you should market them. Likewise, there are many companies with open positions that may not fit your skills. You need to spend time matching your key skills with the types of positions that fit your skills.

Action Steps for You:

1. Review the skills list developed during your self-assessment.
2. Determine which skills you want to highlight during your search.
3. Determine skills you wish to downplay or ignore, such as any out-of-date skills you may have.
4. Determine which soft skills you need to practice, such as giving speeches or writing reports.
5. Determine which personal skills you want to highlight.
6. Build a SUPER™ story around each key skill (see pages 76–78).
7. Practice your SUPER™ stories. Rehearse them by yourself or tell them to a family member. Practice them until you tell each story naturally.

Additional Action Steps for You to Consider:

1. _____

2. _____

3. _____

4. _____

5. _____

SUPER™ Stories

All of us have had experiences during our working lives in which we have successfully used the skills that we developed. For each of us those events and experiences are chapters and stories in our *book of life*. You need to learn how to tell these stories when you are being interviewed for a job.

Think of a time during your childhood when your parents, grandparents, or favorite uncle or aunt told you about how things were when they were growing up or about incidents or experiences from their lives. I am sure you responded—when they had finished—by saying that you really liked their stories. In reality, the only thing that your loved ones did was to create pictures in your mind of chapters in *their* books of life. You listened attentively because you liked stories.

Actually, *everyone* likes stories.

And *everyone* includes your interviewer. So, shouldn't you tell your interviewer stories about your experiences? Shouldn't you tell him or her about chapters in your book of life that pertain to your work experiences? Shouldn't you tell stories that demonstrate how your skills align with the requirements of the open position? Shouldn't you be creating pictures in his or her mind that convince this person that you are the right applicant for the job?

Of course you should!

I have created a format for you to develop your stories. Each story should be no more than one to two paragraphs long. You should develop a story for each of the skills you identified when assessing yourself. You will tell your stories when you are being interviewed. During the interview, you will be asked a series of questions. You should answer the questions by selecting the most appropriate story to describe to an interviewer your qualifications for the position. You need to create a picture in their mind that demonstrates how you can fulfill the requirements of their position. They will remember your stories similarly to the way you remembered your family's stories. Since they will remember your stories, they will also remember you! Yes, they will remember you above all the other people that applied for the same position ... but did not tell them SUPER™ stories!

SUPER™ is an acronym that stands for:

State of Affairs
Understanding
Power
Execution
Results

State of Affairs

This is where you describe the state of affairs or what created the situation, such as a problem, crisis, event, or opportunity that existed. This section describes the who, what, when, and where. You need to answer these questions:

What was the problem, crisis, event, or opportunity?
What was the environment like in which this situation existed?

Understanding

Here you describe your personal understanding of what should have been done to satisfy the event that you described above. You need to answer the questions:

What was your understanding of what needed to be done to satisfy the situation?
How did you plan to approach the resolution?

Power

This section describes for the interviewer the amount of power that you had to solve this event. This part of the story is designed to demonstrate your independence. You should answer the questions:

How much control did you have over the resolution of the problem?
How much independence did you have during the resolution of the situation?

Execution

Here is where you describe the actions that you took to resolve the event, explaining the step-by-step execution of the approach you followed. This area will contain the most sentences in your story. This is where you create the detailed picture in the interviewer's mind of how you solved a situation using the same skills required for the position for which you are interviewing. This section of the story should answer the questions:

What specific steps did you take to solve the problem?
In what sequence did you take those steps?

Results

This section is probably the most important. Here is where you describe the final result of your actions. This should be a very succinct closing to your story that answers the questions:

What was the final outcome of your actions?
What happened as a result of you executing your step-by-step approach?

You need to create and write down a story for each of your key skills. These are the skills you plan to market during your job search. Once they are written, you should continually practice telling the stories until they flow from you naturally. By naturally, I mean you don't sound like you are reading them from a book. You should practice in front of a mirror, your friends, your spouse, and, if they will sit still long enough, your pet!

I am often asked how long one should practice his or her stories. The answer is simple. You should practice as long as it takes for you to tell your story as naturally as if you were delivering it to a loved one. If there are funny parts, you should naturally smile or lightly chuckle when you tell them. If there are serious parts, then your facial expressions should reveal that fact. The tone of your voice should change as it would if you were telling a family member the story. It should flow from your lips naturally. It should flow naturally, because it is *your* life experience!

Step 3
Develop Your Plan
Task 2: Industries to Research

Chance favors the prepared mind.

—Louis Pasteur

Search for the Best Industry

People would like to believe that most things happen by chance. However, the "chances" that happen to successful people were usually planned by them. They developed plans and executed them. They were mentally prepared to handle anything that attempted to interfere with the successful execution of their plans.

In your plan, you should be prepared to search for a position in those industries that can use your specific skills. That will significantly increase the probability of your success in finding the right job.

Action Steps for You:

1. List the industries that can best use your skills.
2. List the companies that *might* be able to use your skills.
3. Highlight the selected companies that are close to your location.
4. Determine which companies you are willing to travel to.
5. Determine which companies you are *not* willing to travel to.

Additional Action Steps for You to Consider:

1. _____
   _____

2. _____
   _____

3. _____
   _____

4. _____
   _____

5. _____
   _____

Step 3
Develop Your Plan
Task 3: Companies to Research

*Research your idea. See if there's a demand. A lot of
people have great ideas, but they don't know if there's a
need for it. You also have to research your competition.*

—Magic Johnson

Search for the Best Company

The amount of research that you do will directly affect the level of
success that you achieve. It is not okay to merely have an *idea* about the
industries and companies that can use your talent. You must research
the specific types of companies that are in your selected industries. You
need to match your skills with those companies. This process will make
it easier to convince hiring managers that you are the right person for
their open positions.

Action Steps for You:

1. Review the list of industries selected in task 2 on the previous
    page.
2. List the types of companies in the industries that you selected.
3. List the types of companies in the industries that *might* fit your
    skills.
4. Select your most desired type of company from the list created in
    action step 3 above.

Additional Action Steps for You to Consider:

1. _____
   _____

2. _____
   _____

3. _____
   _____

4. _____
   _____

5. _____
   _____

Step 3
Develop Your Plan
Task 4: Search Firms to Research

It is a good morning exercise for a research scientist to discard a pet hypothesis every day before breakfast.

—Konrad Lorenz

Using Search Firms

There are hundreds of search firms in the staffing and recruiting industry. Job seekers tend to want to send their resumes to all of them. Each believes it will increase his or her probability of getting a job. If you are someone who believes that hypothesis, you may want to discard it. Many search firms specialize in particular industries or skill areas (for example, information technology). You need to determine if there are search firms that specialize in your industry or skill area. Target those firms to help you. They will be knowledgeable both about the industry as well as which companies can use your talents.

Action Steps for You:

1. Make a list of search firms that specialize in your industry.
2. Make a list of executive-recruiting firms.
3. Ensure that these search and executive-recruiting firms are reputable.
4. Make a list of search-firm websites.
5. Sign up for electronic alerts on the search websites.
6. Make a list of job-placement agencies.
7. Determine which job-placement agencies you will use when you execute your plan.

Additional Action Steps for You to Consider:

1. _____
   _____
2. _____
   _____
3. _____
   _____
4. _____
   _____
5. _____
   _____

Step 3
Develop Your Plan
Task 5: Personal-Network Contacts

Life is a network of invisible threads!

—Unknown

Creating a Personal Network

You know or have access to more people than you think. It has been said that you are only six levels away from anyone on the planet. That means that you know someone who knows someone who knows someone, and so on, for six levels. These relationships are like an invisible thread that connects everyone. Each of those connections can possibly help you find employment. You need to go where they are and meet them. You need to tell them about your favorite product "brand"—You.

You need to develop a couple of paragraphs about yourself, as if "You" were a brand. It should contain your major strong points from your list of strengths. Memorize what you have written and be prepared to share this information with your personal network. This becomes information they can share when they are describing you to others.

Action Steps for You:

1. Develop a skill for making small talk for use at networking sessions.
2. List your personal network from your assessment.
3. List associations to join.
4. List online social networks to join.
5. List people you want to develop relationships with.
6. Create the You brand language to share with your personal network.

Additional Action Steps for You to Consider:

1. _____
   _____

2. _____
   _____

3. _____
   _____

4. _____
   _____

5. _____
   _____

Step 3
Develop Your Plan
Task 6: Set Daily Action Goals

*In business, I've discovered that my purpose is to do my
best to my utmost ability every day. That's my standard.
I learned early in my life that I had high standards.*

—Donald Trump

Establishing Daily Goals

You need to do something each day toward your goal of finding
employment. You should set that as your standard. The best way to
ensure that you are doing something each day is to prepare a daily plan.
This is a step-by-step set of activities that will continuously move you
closer to your goal. One of the most important activities that you should
plan is "free time." Your free-time activities are just as important as all
of the other actions that will help you to be successful; they help you to
clear your mind and recharge your internal batteries.

Action Steps for You:

1. Review the Self-Marketing-Plan Checklist (see next page).
2. Determine the number of personal contacts you will call each day
   (about five to ten).
3. Determine the number of companies you will contact each day.
4. Determine the number of follow-up contacts you will complete
   each day.
5. Determine the number of resumes you will send each day.
6. Determine how much time will be allocated to computer
   searches.
7. Determine the number of phone calls you will make each day.
8. Determine how much free time you will allocate each day.

Additional Action Steps for You to Consider:

1. _____
   _____
2. _____
   _____
3. _____
   _____
4. _____
   _____

Self-Marketing Plan Checklist
To be completed daily to achieve my goals

Personal Contacts *(Whom do I plan to contact?)*:		
	☐	
	☐	
	☐	
	☐	
	☐	
	☐	
	☐	
Companies to Contact:		
	☐	
	☐	
	☐	
	☐	
	☐	
	☐	
	☐	
Associations to Contact:		
	☐	
	☐	
	☐	
	☐	
	☐	
	☐	
	☐	
Social Media Contacts *(Whom do I plan to contact)*:		
	☐	
	☐	
	☐	
	☐	
	☐	
	☐	
Amount of Free Time Today:		
	☐	30 mins	
	☐	45 mins	
	☐	1 hour	
	☐	1½ hours	
	☐	2 hours	

Step 4
Final Review of Your Plan
Task 1: Develop Plan Checklist

*I learned to embrace risk, as long as it was well thought out
and, in a worst-case scenario, I'd still land on my feet.*

—Eli Broad

Developing a Plan Checklist

Successful people know exactly what they need to do each day to be and remain successful. Their actions are well thought out. The most important aspect of their behavior, however, is that they write down what they need to do. They will then move toward their goals each day. This helps them to deal calmly with the obstacles that are inevitably going to get in their way. They categorize and review every phase of what needs to be done and the sequence in which to do it. They check off each item as it is completed.

Action Steps for You:

1. Complete the Self-Marketing-Plan Checklist.
2. Complete the personal-contacts category of the checklist.
3. Complete the company category of the checklist.
4. Complete the association category of the checklist.
5. Complete the social-media-contacts category of the checklist.
6. Complete the personal-free-time category of the checklist.

Additional Action Steps for You to Consider:

1. _____
   _____
2. _____
   _____
3. _____
   _____
4. _____
   _____
5. _____
   _____

Step 4
Final Review of Your Plan
Task 2: All Steps Covered

*I have not failed. I have found ten
thousand ways that won't work.*

—Thomas A. Edison

Reviewing All Plan Steps

It is extremely important that you check every aspect of your plan. You may review something that you created a few days ago ... or maybe a week ago. A review of your plan will help you to see some aspect of your plan that just won't work. This is the time to add, remove, or update any area that may be in question. For example, you may have noticed that you missed planning to attend some networking sessions; add them to your plan right away. It will be more difficult to make adjustments while you are executing your plan.

You need to look for gaps in your plan. It is essential that you discover and correct them before executing your plan. It is easy to forget to develop a SUPER™ story for a skill, especially a skill that you added to your assessment after you completed writing the initial stories. Likewise, you may talk to someone who reminds you of a company to pursue, but you might forget to capture it in your plan if you don't have it with you at the time. The key is to discover your gaps now. You need to double-check your plan now—*before* you execute it.

Action Steps for You:

1. Ensure that you have documented all your key skills.
2. Ensure you have a SUPER™ story for each of your key skills.
3. Ensure that you have documented key industries.
4. Verify that you have a solid list of companies to pursue.
5. Put together a solid list of social-media websites to join.
6. Ensure that you have many copies of your daily checklist.

Additional Action Steps for You to Consider:

1. _____
   _____
2. _____
   _____
3. _____
   _____
4. _____
   _____
5. _____
   _____

Step 4
Final Review of Your Plan
Task 3: Test the Plan

*Experience enables you to recognize a
mistake when you make it again.*

—Franklin P. Jones

Practice Your Plan

It is time to test the plan. You need to gain a lot of experience by testing
your plan over and over again. The time to learn what areas to improve
is while you are practicing everything. You need to practice writing your
resume and cover letter, telling your stories, selecting industries and
companies, and finally, contacting companies. These practice sessions
will help you to feel comfortable and natural when you are executing
your plan. And who knows? Your practice company may decide to hire
you!

Action Steps for You:

1. Review your resume with someone you trust.
2. Review your SUPER™ story with someone you trust.
3. Rehearse your SUPER™ story with someone you trust.
4. Rehearse your SUPER™ story in front of the mirror.
5. Select an industry and *one* company in the industry.
6. Research the specifics of the company.
7. Send the company your resume and cover letter.

Additional Action Steps for You to Consider:

1. _____
   _____
2. _____
   _____
3. _____
   _____
4. _____
   _____
5. _____
   _____

Step 4
Final Review of Your Plan
Task 4: Make Adjustments

Being defeated is often a temporary condition.
Giving up is what makes it permanent.

—Marilyn vos Savant

Adjusting Your Plan

You need to make adjustments after you get a response from your test company. A rejection is not a defeat—it is a learning experience. Determine if you need to make adjustments. Review your cover letter. Ensure that it briefly introduces you and asks for an appointment. Ensure that your resume clearly describes your work experience. Of course, you may have had the opportunity to use your stories. Ensure that they are crisp and to the point.

Action Steps for You:

1. Analyze the test company response. (Select a new test company if you don't receive any response.)
2. Adjust your cover letter if necessary.
3. Adjust your resume if necessary.
4. Adjust any SUPER™ stories if necessary.
5. Adjust your industry and company lists if necessary.

Additional Action Steps for You to Consider:

1. _____
   _____

2. _____
   _____

3. _____
   _____

4. _____
   _____

5. _____
   _____

EXECUTING YOUR PLAN

Overview: Making It Happen

Now that you have developed your plan, the next thing to do is to execute it. The objective of this chapter is to assist you in executing your plan.

As stated earlier, the people you know and the people they know will help you to advance your career, so I will work with you on how to generate leads. Making contact is only the first step, however. It is important to know how to make contact and what to do once you have made contact. You also need to follow up with both the person you spoke with and the person who gave you the referral.

Making contact with people who can help you be successful in finding a job is called networking. I will show you places where you can network to meet the people who may be valuable to you. These will be people who can help you to achieve your goal.

When you meet people in a networking environment, you need to communicate your brand. Companies brand their most important products. They create a memorable image of each of their products so that you will remember it when you are ready to make a purchase. You also need to market your most important product: you! You will need to establish a "You" brand just like companies do with their products. I will show you how to develop a memorable image for your brand.

While networking, you will need to quickly communicate your brand. You will learn to do this with an elevator speech. This technique will allow you to quickly present your most important features in a short period of time. This is similar to what a company does with a thirty-second commercial. In many cases, however, you won't have thirty seconds, so it is imperative that you are focused in both your content and delivery.

When we are children, we hear a lot of stories. Some stories are from storybooks like *Alice in Wonderland*, which I mentioned in the previous chapter. Many stories are about our families; we hear these stories from our parents, grandparents, and other relatives. The thing that makes stories so special to us is that we remember them regardless of how we learn about them.

In the previous chapter you developed SUPER™ stories about

yourself. In this chapter, you will practice telling at least one SUPER™ story each day. You will rehearse them over and over until they come out as naturally as when your grandparents told their stories. You will practice your stories so that they will be both interesting and memorable. You will learn to tell a SUPER™ story in two to three minutes. Your objective is to make your interviews memorable by telling an interesting SUPER™ story at the appropriate time.

Finally, I will show you how to approach the companies that you previously selected. You will approach companies that have the cultures, values, locations, and benefits that are consistent with yours. The objective is to not just find a job but to build a career with a company with which you are very comfortable.

Step 1
Making Contact
Task 1: Lead Generation

The reverse side also has a reverse side.

—Japanese Proverb

Generating Leads

A key objective in developing a job-search strategy is to create an unlimited supply of names. Many of the social networks can help you accomplish this task. When you determine which companies you would like to pursue, you can search the social networks for employees within those companies. In contacting the individuals within those companies, you will eventually establish relationships with them. Even if you do not end up working for those companies, your new relationships within those companies can provide you with additional contacts. It is like looking at the reverse side of the reverse side.

Action Steps for You:

1. Look up target-company employees in social-network websites.
2. Connect with target-company employees via these social networks.
3. Send target-company employees letters or e-mails based on a template.
4. Get the names of potential contacts from family members and friends.
5. Get the names of potential contacts from acquaintances.
6. Contact the people whose names were provided by family, friends, and acquaintances.

Additional Action Steps for You to Consider:

1. _____
   _____

2. _____
   _____

3. _____
   _____

4. _____
   _____

5. _____
   _____

Step 1
Making Contact
Task 2: Create Personal Note Cards

*Everyone thinks of changing the world, but
no one thinks of changing themselves.*

—Leo Tolstoy

Personal Notes

A number of people will help you with your job-search campaign. It is imperative that you develop the habit of thanking them for their support. An effective method of thanking people is to send personal, handwritten notes. Performing this act may be new to you, but that is something that you will need to change. Be prepared to send a thank-you note after someone does something to help your job search effort. For example, if a friend provides you with the contact information for a hiring manager and you get an interview, you should send a personal note to your friend. It is an effective way of maintaining support during your job-search campaign. In addition, you should always have business cards. You should give one of your business cards to every individual that you meet for the first time. This is a good way for people to remember you. Be careful not to send too many to the same person. That could become annoying. Plan to take the person to lunch or coffee if they have given you a great deal of support.

Action Steps for You:

1. Make or buy personal note cards.
2. Make a list of *close* personal contacts who can assist you.
3. Make or buy return address labels.
4. Make or buy simple personal business cards.

Additional Action Steps for You to Consider:

1. _____
   _____

2. _____
   _____

3. _____
   _____

Step 1
Making Contact
Task 3: Create a Personal-Letter Template

You can't build a reputation on what you are going to do.
—Henry Ford

Personal Letters:

One of the key actions you should take is developing personal letters to friends, family members, acquaintances, and anyone who can assist you in finding a job. Send them a brief letter explaining your situation. You will develop a reputation for being brave enough to allow people who are close to you to help. You will be surprised how much it will be appreciated.

Action Steps for You:

1. Create a letter template to personal acquaintances.
2. Make a letter template for people referred to you by others.
3. Make a letter or e-mail template for target-company employees who can help you.
4. Make a template for close friends who can help.

Additional Action Steps for You to Consider:

1. _____
   _____
2. _____
   _____
3. _____
   _____
4. _____
   _____
5. _____
   _____

Step 1
Making Contact
Task 4: Learn How to Grow from Contacts

We find comfort among those who agree with us—growth among those who don't.

—Frank A. Clark

Learning from Contacts

You need to personally meet and talk with everyone who could possibly help you. Tell them your situation. Explain the approach you are using to find employment. Ask them for their opinions on how you should proceed. Ask them whom they recommend you contact. And then *be quiet and listen.* It will feel extremely comfortable when they agree with everything you are doing. It will feel very uncomfortable when they don't. Listen anyway. You may learn something that will help you to grow in this endeavor. For example, they may tell you that you don't listen well. This could impact your ability to interview well. In that case, you should practice listening, take a course on listening, or find a book on developing listening skills. Your growth in that area can lead to success in your job search.

Action Steps for You:

1. Meet and talk to key family members.
2. Meet with close friends.
3. Meet with key acquaintances.
4. Personally meet as many employees as possible in the target company.
5. Personally meet anyone whose name you were given.
6. Listen to and follow up on any advice that they give you.

Additional Action Steps for You to Consider:

1. _____
   _____
2. _____
   _____
3. _____
   _____

Step 1
Making Contact
Task 5: Post-Appointment Notes

There is no limit to what you can do if
you don't care who gets the credit.

—Unknown

Capturing Key Ideas

You will meet many new people as a result of the contacts that your network will provide you. Some of the people will simply be connections to other people who can help; in other cases, you will meet hiring managers and decision makers. Regardless of who they are, it is important that you record the results of those meetings. These recordings are called post-appointment notes. These notes contain the key points shared with you during the meeting and will become especially important if a person was not comfortable with you taking notes during your meeting. In some cases, the venue or place where you held the meeting (such as a park bench) was just not conducive to writing and talking. In any case, it is imperative that you remember what was discussed. The post-appointment notes will help you remember.

Action Steps for You:

1. Write down key ideas from each meeting.
2. Separate your notes into categories.
3. File your notes neatly for further reference.
4. Check your notes periodically for key ideas.
5. Send thank-you notes to the people who helped you make these contacts.

Additional Action Steps for You to Consider:

1. _____
   _____

2. _____
   _____

3. _____
   _____

4. _____
   _____

Step 2
Power Networking
Task 1: Join and Participate in Organizations

There's a fine line between participation and mockery.

—Scott Adams

Joining Organizations

You need to attend as many functions and events as you can. The chambers of commerce in many cities have business-networking events. In addition, many industry associations hold periodic networking sessions. People get to know each other and exchange business cards at these gatherings. The most important aspect of these events is that people can connect you with other people who may be able to help your situation.

Find out when these functions occur and arrange your calendar to attend them. Occasionally, you may need to literally go from one event to the next. Once there, participate. That means you need to make it a point to meet as many people as you can. You are simply making a mockery of your job-search efforts if you attend these events and don't participate in the networking activities.

Action Steps for You:

1. Attend chamber of commerce networking events.
2. Attend free business seminars.
3. Attend trade-association functions.
4. Attend regional meet-and-greet events.
5. Attend political meet-and-greet events.
6. Look for *hidden* positions in companies and organizations.
7. Volunteer in these organizations whenever possible.

Additional Action Steps for You to Consider:

1. _____
   _____

2. _____
   _____

3. _____
   _____

4. _____
   _____

Step 2
Power Networking
Task 2: The 4 P's of Marketing

*The best thing about the future is that
it comes one day at a time.*

—Abraham Lincoln

Marketing Yourself

Marketing professionals focus on something called the 4 P's: product, promotion, price, and place. Marketing people develop a strategy for each of these items in order to market their products. Your product is *you*. You need to determine the future of your product. Develop an understanding of each of 4 P's as it relates to your product. Your strategy should be to consistently market your product one day at a time.

Let's discuss each of the P's, starting with product. For our purposes, the product is you. In the next section we will discuss elevator speeches. (You should develop an elevator speech that contains important information about your strongest skills.) This will be a clear definition of your product.

The next P is promotion. This simply means taking full advantage of every opportunity to tell people about yourself and your marketable skills. You should plan to attend networking events; make appointments with people who can help you fulfill your job-search objectives; and follow up on contacts that were provided to you by your network. This may be uncomfortable at first, but you need to try to benefit from every chance you get to tell someone about yourself. Successful job searchers do it all the time.

The next P is price. The marketing professional ensures that the price of his or her product is set at a level at which people will buy it. You will be asked your salary range. This is your price. Many job seekers will set a high range expecting to cover the amounts they "lost" during unemployment. Some will set it too low based on a feeling of desperation. You need to understand the current salary ranges that exist for your skills. You can uncover this information by searching the Internet, looking at company job websites, or asking someone in the recruiting field. Then, when asked about your salary requirements, you can present a price for your product that people will buy.

The last P is place. Marketing people ensure that they place their products in locations where their target markets will buy them. For example, tractors are generally sold in areas that have a number of farms. Marketers know that their target market is not located in the cities. You need to make sure that if you have a unique skill, which is specific to a particular industry, you position yourself as often as possible around that industry. For example, I coached a person from the automobile manufacturing industry. We decided that he should only attend networking sessions in cities where there were automobile manufacturers. This approach both optimized his networking time and put him close to his target market.

Ensure that you execute the steps in your plan that take advantage of the 4 P's.

Action Steps for You:

1. Determine where your target industries are located.
2. Attend chamber of commerce or business-networking events in those locations.
3. Attend industry business-networking events in those locations.
4. Send your resume to the companies in your target industries that utilize your skills.
5. Determine the current salary range for your skills in your target industries.

Additional Action Steps for You to Consider:

1. _____
   _____
2. _____
   _____
3. _____
   _____
4. _____
   _____
5. _____
   _____

Step 2
Power Networking
Task 3: Market the "You" Brand

Your premium brand had better be delivering something special, or it's not going to get the business.

—Warren Buffett

Developing Your Brand

In the previous section we discussed the 4 P's of marketing. Now we will get specific about how to develop the brand for your product.

Every company has a premium brand that they market. For example, the Coca-Cola Company has its Coke brand for its soft drink products. They believe that their brand delivers something special. You have the "You" brand for your product. Make sure that you can articulate what makes your brand special.

You need to develop an elevator speech for your brand. Imagine that you enter an elevator on the ground floor with someone that you absolutely know can get you a job. Both of you are going to the tenth floor. You need to develop a speech that you can deliver to that person before the elevator reaches the tenth floor. That means you must be able to deliver what is special about your brand in about thirty seconds.

Action Steps for You:

1. Tell people about your key competencies.
2. Create your elevator speech
3. Tell people about your significant traits.
4. Tell people about your unique knowledge.
5. Highlight the key aspects of your personality.

Additional Action Steps for You to Consider:

1. _____
   _____
2. _____
   _____
3. _____
   _____
4. _____
   _____

Step 2
Power Networking
Task 4: Refine Your SUPER™ Stories

Aim for the top. There is plenty of room there.
There are so few at the top it is almost lonely there.

—Samuel Insull

Refining Your Stories

You have already decided to move yourself above the rest of the job searching pack by following the techniques in this book; you will make it to the top of the pack by achieving success in your job search. One of the techniques that will help you achieve that success is practicing your SUPER™ stories over and over. You want to practice them so much that you can just naturally discuss them as though you were telling a friend an interesting story. Practicing your SUPER™ stories now will also increase your comfort level when you are telling them during an interview. Refine your stories as needed to ensure that you feel comfortable with the details.

Action Steps for You:

1.   Select one SUPER™ story to practice each day.
2.   Select a few close people to listen to you practice your stories.
3.   Practice the selected story multiple times during the day.
4.   Refine any uncomfortable parts of the story.
5.   Repeat practicing the story until it feels natural.

Additional Action Steps for You to Consider:

1. _____

2. _____

3. _____

4. _____

5. _____

Step 3
Researching Companies
Task 1: New Skills Needed in the Field

To avoid criticism, do nothing, say nothing and be nothing.
—Elbert Hubbard

Developing New Skills

Many job seekers will send their resumes to a large number of companies not knowing whether or not their skills are needed. You must match your skills with the needs of the industries that you select. This may mean that you need to develop some new skills that enhance your current skills. For example, you may learn that there is a new programming language that is needed in the information technology industry. Maybe you already know how to program but just don't know this particular language. You need to find out the best way to learn this new language and increase your probability of getting hired.

Determine how to enhance your skills to match the industry needs. Make a SUPER™ story for your skills that matches these needs. Develop a plan to acquire the skills that you are missing. Once acquired, develop SUPER™ stories for those skills as well.

Action Steps for You:

1. Determine which skills are in demand in the industry.
2. Determine how to acquire skills you are missing that are in demand.
3. Match your new skill set with the needed skills.
4. Execute your plan to acquire the missing skills.

Additional Action Steps for You to Consider:

1. _____

_____

2. _____

_____

3. _____

_____

4. _____

_____

5. _____

_____

Step 3
Researching Companies
Task 2: Companies Needing Skills

If everyone is thinking alike, then somebody isn't thinking.

—George S. Patton

Developing a List of Companies

Now that you have matched your skills with the industry skills that are needed, you need to find the companies in that industry. One technique for finding a company in your selected industries is to look up that company on a government website such as the Bureau of Labor Statistics site. Obtain the company's NAICS (North American Industry Classification System) code and search for all of the other companies that have that same code. This will give you an immediate list of companies that you can target. You are not thinking like everyone else when you put approaches like this in your job search plan. Think of a number of other things like this that you can do.

Action Steps for You:

1. Review newspaper articles highlighting the companies on your list, as well as the companies' want ads.
2. Search for job fairs in area.
3. Review magazine articles about companies.
4. Search job websites for companies needing your skills.
5. Select the companies in the industry that demand your skills.
6. Categorize the companies by which of your skills are needed.
7. Create a list of target companies to pursue.
8. Practice those of your SUPER™ stories that are tied to the skills needed.

Additional Action Steps for You to Consider:

1. _____
   _____

2. _____
   _____

3. _____
   _____

4. _____
   _____

Step 3
Researching Companies
Task 3: Company Information

Be not simply good—be good for something.

—Henry David Thoreau

Gathering Knowledge About Companies

Find out everything that you can about the companies that you select. The Internet can provide you with a great deal of information that previously was unavailable; this will help you to determine if the selected companies meet your criteria. You will become extremely enthusiastic about a company the more you learn about it. That enthusiasm will generate excitement. You will learn why you are good for that company and why that company is good for you. Your knowledge of the company and your enthusiasm about it will project itself during the interview. Wouldn't you want to hire someone that was enthusiastic about working with you?

Action Steps for You:

1. Get publicly available information.
2. Review companies' websites.
3. Retrieve as much information as possible from websites that can help you.
4. Determine the location of the company.
5. Determine company size (in sales dollars and employees).
6. Classify each company by industry.
7. Further refine your target company list.

Additional Action Steps for You to Consider:

1. _____
   _____
2. _____
   _____
3. _____
   _____
4. _____
   _____
5. _____
   _____

Step 3
Researching Companies
Task 4: Key People in Company

Don't tell people how to do things, tell them what to do and let them surprise you with their results.

—George S. Patton

Researching Key People

It is extremely important to know something about the people who manage the company. The personality of the leadership team directly or indirectly impacts the attitudes of the employees; therefore, you need to research the backgrounds of the company's leadership team. It is equally important to know something about the hiring manager if you are pursuing a specific job. This will help you to understand this person's management style. There also may be other people that are currently in the company that can help you.

You can generally research information about these people on the company website. Most companies (especially companies on the stock exchange) have a section of their website that describes the management people. It will provide biographical information as well.

You can search the Internet for individuals who do not appear on the company website. Many people in the business world have at least one profile on one of the social media websites (such as LinkedIn). Professionals may include biographical entries on these websites that will give you some insight into their backgrounds.

Action Steps for You:

1. Learn about the chief executive officer (CEO).
2. Learn about the president and chief operating officer (COO).
3. Learn about the head of human resources.
4. Learn about the hiring manager (if known).
5. Learn about the head of finance.
6. Find any additional company employees who can help you.

Additional Action Steps for You to Consider:

1. _____

2. _____

3. _____

4. _____

5. _____

Step 3
Researching Companies
Task 5: Target Companies

The only test of leadership is that somebody follows.

—Robert K. Greenleaf

Using a Company's Website

Many companies now place their open positions directly on their websites. This helps them to avoid the expense of using recruiting agencies. This can also help you later when you are negotiating your compensation. You should look on each target company's website to find positions that match your skills. Often you can apply directly on the company's website for these positions. Keep a log of the company sites that you have visited and whether or not you applied for any positions. Keep copies of the descriptions of the position for which you apply. Also keep track of which version of your resume you sent. You should record this information in your Log of Company Websites Visited (*see* page 134). This will help you if the opportunity for an interview arises.

Action Steps for You:

1. Check company websites for open positions.
2. Prepare *tailored* cover letters for all open positions.
3. Prepare *tailored* resumes for all open positions.
4. Apply for open positions online if possible.
5. Send resumes and cover letters for all open positions.
6. Repeat this process for all selected companies.
7. Each day review the status of positions that you applied for online.

Additional Action Steps for You to Consider:

1. _____

2. _____

3. _____

4. _____

5. _____

LOG OF COMPANY WEBSITE VISITS

#	Company Name	Open Positions (Y/N)	Applied for Position (Y/N)	Date Applied	Sent Cover Letter (Y/N)	Sent Resume (Y/N)	Received Reply From Company? (Y/N)	Resume File on My Computer
1	Company AAA	Y	Y	10/1/2009	Y	Y	Y	C:/Documents/Myresumes/companyaaa.doc
2	Company BBB	N	Y	11/15/2009	Y	Y	Y	C:/Documents/Myresumes/companybbb.doc
3	Company CCC	Y	Y	1/20/2010	Y	Y		C:/Documents/Myresumes/companyccc.doc
4	Company DDD	N	N	n/a	N	N		
5	Company XYZ	Y	Y	2/10/2010	Y	Y		C:/Documents/Myresumes/companyxyz.doc
6	Company WXY	N	Y	2/10/2010	Y	Y		C:/Documents/Myresumes/companywxy.doc
7	Company EEE	Y	Y	3/15/2010	Y	Y		C:/Documents/Myresumes/companyeee.doc
8	Company NNN	N	N	n/a	N	N		
9	Company GGG	Y	Y	3/15/2010	Y	Y		C:/Documents/Myresumes/companyggg.doc
10	Company ZZZ	Y	Y	3/15/2010	Y	Y		C:/Documents/Myresumes/companyzzz.doc

You may want to send your resume to a company even if they don't currently have an open position.

WAYNE'S TIPS
You should consider adding additonal columns such as:

-- Date Company Replied
-- Date Follow-Up Note Sent
-- Interview (Y/N)
-- Job Offer (Y/N)

Page 1 of 1

Step 4
Selecting the Right Company
Task 1: Company Culture

*Choose a job you love, and you will never
have to work a day in your life.*

—Confucius

Match the Company's Values

It is just as important for you to find the *right* company as it is for the company to find the right employee. You need to choose the company that is the right fit as well as the job that is the right one. You will love going to work each day if you find the right match. Of course, the things that make it the right company usually have to do with company culture. This is something that you can't see or touch—it just is. The culture has a great deal to do with the company's values, so you need to work as hard as you can to learn the company's values. It is extremely important that the company's values match your values. You will never feel like you are going to work each day when there is a match between your values and your company's.

Action Steps for You:

1. Find any information you can about the company's culture.
2. Read the company's mission statement on their website.
3. Determine if information exists about the company's values.
4. Determine if the company's culture matches your values.
5. Read articles that provide insight into the company's values.

Additional Action Steps for You to Consider:

1. _____
   _____

2. _____
   _____

3. _____
   _____

4. _____
   _____

5. _____
   _____

Step 4
Selecting the Right Company
Task 2: Company Benefits

*I conceive that knowledge of books is the basis
on which all other knowledge rests.*

—George Washington

Understanding Company Benefits

You will need to fund any benefit that is not provided by the company, so it is extremely important that you understand the benefits that the company provides. You need to know about such things as sick leave, which types of insurance are provided, and pension benefits. Job seekers usually receive this information *after* they have accepted a position with the company. Of course, that is too late. They are sometimes then disappointed or dissatisfied with their decision to join their chosen companies. This is the reason why you need to learn this information *before* you begin work at a company. There are many books available on any benefit topic that you may not understand. The best strategy is for you to understand the company's benefits *before you even begin pursuing employment with them*. In many cases, this information can be found on the company website. You can prevent dissatisfaction later by completing this task first.

There are places where you can find this information other than the company website. For example, you may be able to find a current or former employee who can help you. You can also try to find a recruiting firm that works with your target company. They are usually very familiar with the benefits of the companies they work with since they have to communicate these details to their clients.

Action Steps for You:

1. Review the company's life insurance options.
2. Review the company's health insurance options.
3. Review the company's dental insurance options.
4. Review information on maternity leave, vacations, sick leave, and personal days.
5. Determine if the benefits match your expectations.
6. Remove any company from the list whose benefits don't match your expectations.

Additional Action Steps for You to Consider:

1. _____
   _____
2. _____
   _____
3. _____
   _____
4. _____
   _____
5. _____
   _____

Step 4
Selecting the Right Company
Task 3: Company Location

I recommend you to take care of the minutes;
the hours will take care of themselves.

—Lord Chesterfield

Understand Your Commute

The extra minutes that you spend commuting to work can add up to hours in your life. That is time that you spend being away from your family, not enjoying your hobbies, and missing the companionship of your closest friends. In the past, I have traveled close to two hours one way to my job; that translates to approximately *a month and a half each year* spent in traffic. You should investigate whether the company has a location closer to where you live. In addition, even if you would not have a long commute, you might determine that the company is in a location where you would rather not go each day. You need to determine if that is important to your decision to work for that company.

Action Steps for You:

1. Determine if the company has multiple locations.
2. Determine if the company has a location that you would like to work in.
3. Determine if your skills are needed in the desired location.
4. Remove from your list companies that are in undesirable locations.

Additional Action Steps for You to Consider:

1. _____

2. _____

3. _____

4. _____

5. _____

Step 4
Selecting the Right Company
Task 4: Company Size

Strong ethical behavior is good business.

—Wayne L. Anderson

Selecting the Right Size Company

You need to determine the size of the company in which you feel the most comfortable. The size could relate to the profits it earns, the number of people it employs, or the number of locations it has. You need to determine which of those aspects is more important to you.

You may like working in a small company rather than a large one or vice versa. You should look at all aspects when determining a company's size. In addition, it is extremely important to know—regardless of the size—whether or not the company is profitable. You don't want to spend a great deal of time pursuing employment in a company only to experience them closing their doors. Often you can find this information through newspaper articles or financial reports. Have someone review the financials with you if you are not familiar with reading these reports. You will have lost valuable time in pursing the company if they are not profitable, as you would have to start your job search all over again. A company with good ethics will communicate that information when asked, but, as mentioned, that information may be available from many other sources, especially if it is a publicly owned company (that is, it is on a stock exchange).

Action Steps for You:

1. Determine the number of employees at the company.
2. Determine the size of the company in sales dollars.
3. Determine whether company has been profitable.
4. Determine your *ideal* company size.
5. Determine whether the company size matches your ideal company size.

Additional Action Steps for You to Consider:

1. _____
   _____
2. _____
   _____
3. _____
   _____
4. _____
   _____
5. _____
   _____

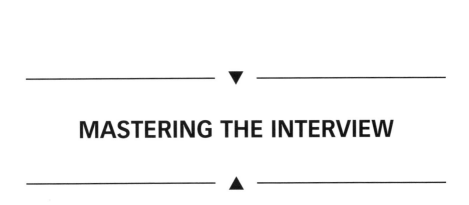

MASTERING THE INTERVIEW

Overview:
Successful Interviewing Techniques

Do you believe that you can control a job interview? Well, contrary to popular belief, you can! The objective of this chapter is to put you in control of your interviews. You will be provided with the knowledge and techniques to ace just about any interview.

First, you will learn about interview mechanics, or the time structure of an interview session. Most interviews last about an hour. The interview does not start the minute you walk in the door; there is time up front to greet your interviewer and other staff, obtain a beverage, hang up your coat, and perform ice-breaking small talk. This generally lasts about five minutes. The end of the interview is pretty much the same, with the addition of closing remarks about next steps, and so on. This also lasts about five minutes. That leaves approximately fifty minutes for the actual interview. You need to realize that, on average, it takes about three to five minutes to ask a question and get a complete answer. Therefore, only about ten to fifteen questions will be asked and answered during an interview session. You and the interviewer have an equal right during the interview to ask questions. In a typical interview session, the interviewer will ask you five to seven questions, and you will ask the interviewer five to seven questions.

Now, here is how you can control the interview: You can generally guess which questions you will be asked since you have probably been interviewed before. You will learn in this chapter the appropriate techniques for preparing answers to those questions. That covers that five to seven questions that the interviewer will ask. Next, you will have prepared five to seven questions that you will ask based on your research of the company. That covers the five to seven questions that you are going to ask. In reality, that means you are prepared to handle *all* of the questions that will be asked during the interview session. In most cases, the interviewer is going to be as nervous about the interview as you are. So, in reality, who is actually controlling the interview? That's right—you are!

In this chapter, I will also teach you how to learn about your interviewer. Many people these days post profiles on social-networking sites. This information is generally available to the public. Some restrict viewing of their profiles to just their professional connections or friends. If this is the case, join the social networking site and connect with the interviewer. You can even begin to exchange information *before* you have the interview. It will be like you are old friends by the time you actually have the interview!

In this chapter I will also talk with you about understanding the interview venue. Know the location of your interview and practice going there if possible. Nothing tells more about your character and work habits as arriving at an interview on time or, better yet, a little early.

Finally, I will cover the most important topic in this book: how to ace the interview!

Step 1
Understand Interview Mechanics
Task 1: Active Listening

Silence is the ultimate weapon of power.

—Charles de Gaulle

Good Listening Skills

You send out your resume and cover letter in order to get an interview. The objective of the interview is to get the job! Therefore, the interview is the most important aspect of all your job-search activities. You must understand the mechanics of the interview process. Be prepared to answer questions using your SUPER™ stories. Most important, however, is that you learn to be a good listener. Keep silent while the interviewer is talking. Learn active listening techniques to ensure the interviewer knows that you are interested. Make sure that you have practiced your SUPER™ stories so that your responses are interesting. Be sure that your interview is memorable.

Action Steps for You:

1. Understand that interviews usually last an hour.
2. Understand that the first five minutes are generally introductions.
3. Understand that the last five minutes are usually reserved for wrap-up.
4. Understand that approximately ten to fifteen questions will be asked and answered.
5. Be prepared to *answer* five to seven questions.
6. Be prepared to *ask* five to seven questions.

Additional Action Steps for You to Consider:

1. _____
   _____
2. _____
   _____
3. _____
   _____
4. _____
   _____
5. _____
   _____

Step 1
Understand Interview Mechanics
Task 2: Body Language

Who you are speaks so loud I can't hear what you're saying.

—Ralph Waldo Emerson

Nonverbal Communication

You need to understand that what you don't *say* generally communicates much more than your actual words; this is known as body language—in other words, your facial expressions, gestures, posture, and eye contact are all considered body language. Even how you dress for the interview will communicate more than your words. This all tells the interviewer something about *who* you are. Study body-language techniques. One way to do this is to observe other people in public places. Try to learn something about them without hearing what they are talking about. Of course, you should be discreet. In addition, there are numerous books and articles on the subject.

The reason learning body language is important is that all of these things are also true about the person interviewing you. You will be able to learn about what the interviewer is *not saying* as well. This can help you to determine the best answer to the question, the best SUPER™ story to tell, or the best time to be silent.

Action Steps for You:

1. Sit up straight.
2. Make good eye contact.
3. Use appropriate conversation gestures.
4. Demonstrate good listening skills.
5. Reach out and provide a firm handshake.
6. Smile as pleasantly as you can.
7. Ensure that you are relaxed.
8. Treat telephone interviews like you were face to face.

Additional Action Steps for You to Consider:

1. _____

2. _____

3. _____

4. _____

5. _____

Step 1
Understand Interview Mechanics
Task 3: Questions They Will Ask You

No problem can withstand the assault of sustained thinking.

—Voltaire

The Interviewer's Questions

You have probably participated in the interview process before. If you haven't, you can talk with someone who has. You know from previous interviews that there are usually about ten questions that are always asked. Spend some sustained time thinking of a list of approximately ten questions that you will *probably* be asked during the interview. Prepare answers for each question. Create a SUPER™ story for as many answers as possible. Rehearse answering each question until the answer feels very natural.

These are questions the interviewer may ask:
What do you consider your strengths to be?
Describe two or three major accomplishments you achieved.
What do you consider your weaknesses to be?
Tell me something about yourself.
What are your long-range goals and objectives?
What are your short-range goals and objectives?
What are the most important rewards you expect in your career?
Why did you choose this as a career?
Describe a situation in which you had to work with a difficult person. How did you handle the situation? Is there anything you think you should have done differently?
What motivates you to put forth your greatest effort?
How have you prepared for a career?
What does success mean to you?
How do you plan to make a contribution to our organization?

What qualities do you look for in your manager?

Was there ever an occasion when you disagreed with a manager? Describe how you handled the situation.

What interests you about our products, services, or company?

How do you work under pressure?

Describe a situation in which you worked as part of a team. What role did you take on?

Action Steps for You:

1. List questions you believe the interviewer will *probably* ask you.
2. Prepare answers using appropriate SUPER™ stories.
3. Practice handling difficult questions.
4. Practice answering questions using your stories.
5. Practice, practice, and when you think you are done, practice some more.

Additional Action Steps for You to Consider:

1. _____

2. _____

3. _____

4. _____

5. _____

Step 1
Understand Interview Mechanics
Task 4: Questions You Will Ask Them

*I am always doing that which I cannot do, in
order that I may learn how to do it.*

—Pablo Picasso

Developing Your Questions

You are learning how to control an interview. You have already prepared
for the questions that the interviewer will ask you. Now you need to
prepare questions that you are going to ask the interviewer. You need to
review the information that you obtained from researching the company.
Prepare approximately five to seven open-ended questions that you will
ask the interviewer. Listen carefully to the answers. Occasionally, buried
in the interviewer's answers are opportunities for you to respond with
your SUPER™ stories. In this instance you are, in essence, answering
a question before it is asked. The key is that it is the answer that *you*
wanted the interviewer to hear!

The following are some questions you might ask:
What would you expect the successful candidate for this job to achieve
over the next sixty days? The next ninety days?
What is valued more in this company: individual contributions or
teamwork?
Could you describe the skills and qualities that management values
most in this company?
In your opinion, what does it take to be successful in this company?
What happened to the last person who had this position?
How did the opening for this position come about?
What is acceptable attire at the company?
What opportunities for training and development are available at the
company?

How does this company measure employee performance?

Tell me something about the company management style. Is management very involved in the day-to-day activities, or are they hands-off?

Could you describe in detail the duties of this position?

Below is an example of how an interviewer's answer to a question could provide an opportunity to tell a SUPER™ story. Assume you have a SUPER™ story about your experience working on a team.

Your Question:

What is valued more in this company, individual contributions or teamwork?

Interviewer's Answer:

We clearly value teamwork more. Our work is structured so that people work together in teams. We believe that the results produce a higher-quality product and usually the tasks get completed more quickly.

Your Response to the Answer:

I am so glad you mentioned that because I have had a great deal of experience working in a team environment. For example ... [Use this opportunity to tell your SUPER™ story.]

This approach helps to provide information about yourself and your qualifications that may not have surfaced in the set of questions the interviewer asked. In addition, it turns the session into more of a conversation than an interview. This will put both you and the interviewer more at ease.

Action Steps for You:

1. Make a list of questions about the company.
2. Make a list of questions about the position.
3. Make a list of questions about the interviewer.
4. All questions should be open ended.
5. Keep in mind that open-ended questions start with *who, what, when, why,* or *how.*
6. Ensure your questions are relevant to the open position.

Additional Action Steps for You to Consider:

1. _____
   _____
2. _____
   _____
3. _____
   _____
4. _____
   _____

Step 1
Understand Interview Mechanics
Task 5: Inserting SUPER™ Stories

If people listened to themselves more often, they would talk less.

—Unknown

Using SUPER™ Stories

SUPER™ stories are the most powerful interviewing technique that you will learn. You will have many opportunities to use them during the interview. SUPER™ stories are your way of describing your work experience and skills in a way that the interviewer will both understand and remember. They are powerful because you can also insert one after you have asked the interviewer a question (see the example in step 1, task 4). You should listen intently for opportunities to tell your stories. Make sure you have enough stories so that you don't tell the same one more than once during an interview. Also, ensure that your stories cover a number of different situations. Listen to yourself when you are telling each story to ensure that you sound natural and relaxed. After all, you already *lived* the story you are telling! Practice listening to yourself tell the stories at home. Remember, the more you tell the story, the more natural it will sound.

Action Steps for You:

1. Listen for questions that address one of your skills.
2. Answer the question by inserting the SUPER™ story for that skill.
3. End the story by asking one of your questions.
4. Repeat this process to make the interview more like a *conversation*.
5. Be relaxed when asking and answering questions.

Additional Action Steps for You to Consider:

1. _____

2. _____

3. _____

4. _____

Step 2
Learn Your Interviewer
Task 1: Search the Web

Management is doing things right;
leadership is doing the right things.

—Peter F. Drucker

Understanding Your Interviewer

Nowadays it is not unusual for you to find information about your interviewers on the Internet. There may have been articles written about them, or they might have written articles that are posted online. They may have spoken at trade conferences, in which case their speeches are likely to be accessible online. In addition, some may write blogs. All of these sources and more can give you some insights about the people who will be interviewing you. You should use this information to prepare some of the insightful questions that you will ask your interviewers. You can also look for areas where you and your interviewers have something in common.

Action Steps for You:

1.   Search the Web for information on your interviewer(s).
2.   Look for articles or blog posts by or about them.
3.   Look for any blogs that they may have written.
4.   Look for information about their career progression.
5.   Look for any speeches that they may have given.
6.   Try to find out which associations they belong to.
7.   Look for any areas that you may have in common.

Additional Action Steps for You to Consider:

1. _____
   _____
2. _____
   _____
3. _____
   _____
4. _____
   _____
5. _____
   _____

Step 2
Learn Your Interviewer
Task 2: Search Social-networking sites

*A habit cannot be tossed out the window; it must
be coaxed down the stairs a step at a time.*

—Mark Twain

Interviewer Information on the Web

There are many social-networking sites to which your interviewers
may belong. Get in the habit of searching these sites for information
about them. They may have Facebook or LinkedIn profiles that you
can access and review. You should create a profile on these networks if
you don't already have one. Make sure you connect to or "make friends
with" the people who are interviewing you. You can also use these sites
to introduce yourself *before* the interview. This helps you to establish a
friendship so that the interview is more comfortable for both of you.
In addition, many people have Twitter accounts. You can use these
accounts to follow the interviewer's comments and activities.

Action Steps for You:

1. Find out which social networks they belong to.
2. Get copies of their networking profiles.
3. Join any network that your interviewers are in that you are not
   currently a part of.
4. Attempt to connect with them in their social network.
5. Learn their hobbies and interests if this information is available.

Additional Action Steps for You to Consider:

1. _____
   _____
2. _____
   _____
3. _____
   _____
4. _____
   _____
5. _____
   _____

Step 2
Learn Your Interviewer
Task 3: Select Key Points

Goals create focus.

—Wayne L. Anderson

Developing Interviewer Facts

Your goal should be to learn and understand as much as you can about the interviewer. This will help you make the interview more focused and personal so that it is more like a conversation with a friend. You should look for common *themes* when analyzing your information. Select the key points that make up that theme. Most important, look for interests that the interviewer has that may be similar to yours. You may consider establishing a SUPER™ story that describes your experience in the area where your background, skills, or hobby matches those of the interviewer. Look for more than one area where you can develop a story.

Action Steps for You:

1. Gather the collected interviewer information.
2. Look for similar topics throughout the information.
3. Record that information as key interviewer points.
4. Identify four to five key points about each interviewer.
5. Beware of any *negative* information that you may find.

Additional Action Steps for You to Consider:

1. _____
   _____
2. _____
   _____
3. _____
   _____
4. _____
   _____
5. _____
   _____

Step 2
Learn Your Interviewer
Task 4: Organize Information

*Organize your life around your dreams. You can
then watch them develop and come true.*

—Wayne L. Anderson

Organizing Interviewer Information

Being organized and methodical is powerful. It is important to make personal notes about what you learn about your interviewer; this will help you to achieve things during your job search that others can only dream about. You can use this information later when you write a follow-up note or e-mail to the interviewer. This will make your follow-up notes more personal and memorable. Ensure that you look for key information and skills that may be similar to yours. Write SUPER™ stories (if you don't already have them) that describe your experiences in the areas where your background and skills match the interviewer's background and skills. Determine where in the interview process you will use the stories that you create.

Action Steps for You:

1. Organize the key information into subject topics.
2. Determine which of the interviewer's skills are revealed.
3. Determine if any of the interviewer skills match your skills.
4. Identify which SUPER™ stories match the identified skills.
5. Plan to use those stories during the interview.

Additional Action Steps for You to Consider:

1. _____

2. _____

3. _____

4. _____

5. _____

Step 3
Understand the Venue
Task 1: Interview Location

*The difference between ordinary and
extraordinary is that little extra.*

—Zig Ziglar

The Importance of Punctuality

A person's punctuality can tell you a lot about them. It is a sign that you
respect other people's time. Because this is so important, you need to
spend the *extra* time learning where your interview will take place. Get
familiar with where it is located, the available parking (if applicable),
and the best route to take to arrive on time. If possible, travel to the
location sometime beforehand so that you can get a feel for the travel
time. Travel there during rush hour since there could be a significant
difference in travel time. You may find that getting to the interview
location is difficult. Consider staying overnight with a family member
or friend who lives close to the interview site. This will ensure that you
arrive at the interview both *fresh* and on time.

Action Steps for You:

1. Determine the travel distance.
2. Determine if an overnight stay will be required.
3. Determine if any of your family or friends live in the area.
4. Ask and learn about unique aspects of the town or city where the
   interview will be.
5. Get very familiar with the area.
6. Practice going to location if possible.

Additional Action Steps for You to Consider:

1. _____
   _____
2. _____
   _____
3. _____
   _____
4. _____
   _____
5. _____
   _____

Step 3
Understand the Venue
Task 2: Location Surroundings

*If you are too busy to help those around
you succeed, you're too busy.*

—Unknown

Maximizing Unscheduled Free Time

You may be scheduled to interview with a number of different people, and it is possible that when you arrive, one or more will not be available, which is something that neither you nor the company planned for. As a result, you might find that you have some unscheduled time between interviews. You should spend time learning the area surrounding the interview location *prior* to the scheduled interview date. You will be able to calmly accept the situation and fill in the time. You will appear astute, accommodating, and flexible. In addition, you will help the company succeed in the interviewing process by eliminating what could have been an awkward situation for them. They will remember how flexible you were and believe that you will also be flexible in your work environment.

Action Steps for You:

1. Find coffee shops near the interview location.
2. Find restaurants near the interview location.
3. Find indoor and outdoor rest spots.
4. Determine if parking will be an issue.
5. Bring reading material in case there are breaks in the interview schedule.

Additional Action Steps for You to Consider:

1. _____
   _____

2. _____
   _____

3. _____
   _____

4. _____
   _____

5. _____
   _____

Step 4
Ace the Interview
Task 1: Be Punctual

*Try not to become a man of success but
rather try to become a man of value.*

—Albert Einstein

Arrive on Time for the Interview

As I mentioned earlier, a person's punctuality says a lot about them. Being on time demonstrates one of your values; it shows that you respect the other person and their time. You should always *plan* to arrive at the interview location earlier than the scheduled time. This will ensure that you arrive on time and will also allow you time to get your thoughts together before the interview. That extra time will help you to appear professional and relaxed. Place the interviewer's name and number in your car. A traffic jam could interfere with you arriving on time, but with this information handy you can call the interviewer from your car to let him or her know the situation. They may want to adjust your interview schedule.

Action Steps for You:

1. First impressions count—be a little early.
2. Allow yourself time to relax before interview.
3. Allow a little time to mentally practice your SUPER™ stories.
4. Visualize the interview going perfectly.
5. Bring extra resumes and personal identification.
6. Turn off your cell phone.

Additional Action Steps for You to Consider:

1. _____
   _____
2. _____
   _____
3. _____
   _____
4. _____
   _____
5. _____
   _____

Step 4
Ace the Interview
Task 2: Dress Code

*Farming looks mighty easy when your plow is a pencil
and you're a thousand miles from the cornfield.*

—Dwight D. Eisenhower

Effective Interview Attire

Wearing the proper attire during an interview may not be as easy as it sounds. For example, wearing a business suit to an interview about a position for a construction equipment operator might be a little too much. Of course, shorts and a tee shirt for the same position might not be desirable either. Many people confuse "casual" and "business casual." This is an easy mistake to make since the definition of both could be very different depending on the work environment. *Casual* will usually mean that dungarees are acceptable. Generally when a company states that the dress code is *business casual*, dungarees are not allowed. The best thing to do if you are not sure is to ask. Once you learn the proper business attire for that company location, dress just a little better. The key is to look professional regardless of the position that you are seeking. It will leave a lasting impression on the interviewer.

Action Steps for You:

1. Find out the dress code in advance.
2. Know the difference between casual versus business casual.
3. Dress slightly better than the dress code requires.
4. Pay attention to clothing details (buttons, color coordination, and so on).
5. Avoid wearing anything that will distract the interviewer.

Additional Action Steps for You to Consider:

1. _____
   _____

2. _____
   _____

3. _____
   _____

4. _____
   _____

5. _____
   _____

Step 4
Ace the Interview
Task 3: Communicate Your Skills

*Failure is only the opportunity to begin
again more intelligently.*

—Henry Ford

Delivering Your Stories

Remember, the objective of the interview is to get hired. There is a high likelihood that the other people seeking the same position as you did not read this book, so by now you must know that the most powerful gambit that you have in your bag of tricks is your SUPER™ stories. You have researched the best ones to use, written them down, and rehearsed them; now you need to *deliver* them—and do so in a calm and relaxed manner. You need to talk with the interviewer as though you are sharing an interesting life story with a friend—because that is exactly what you are doing! The primary purpose of telling these stories is to communicate your skills in a positive and ordinary manner. In addition, you want to communicate your strengths and abilities in a memorable fashion.

Action Steps for You:

1. Speak clearly and concisely.
2. Keep responses specific to the questions you are asked.
3. Use appropriate stories to highlight skills being discussed.
4. Learn to praise yourself.
5. Be prepared to tell them why they should hire you.

Additional Action Steps for You to Consider:

1. _____
   _____
2. _____
   _____
3. _____
   _____
4. _____
   _____
5. _____
   _____

Step 4
Ace the Interview
Task 4: Company Facts

*There are three things extremely hard: steel,
a diamond, and to know one's self.*

—Benjamin Franklin

Using Company Information

By now you have developed a great deal of information about the company that has invited you in for an interview. It is time to put that information to work. Review all of the information that you have developed. Begin to formulate questions about the company. These questions will be derived from information that you read but did not understand, points meant to demonstrate that you did your homework about the company, details about the benefits that may not have become clear through your research, and anything else that will express your interest in the company.

Action Steps for You:

1. Learn key facts about the company.
2. Prepare questions about the company that you will ask.
3. Prepare questions about the leaders' management styles.
4. Prepare questions about company objectives.
5. Prepare questions about company values.

Additional Action Steps for You to Consider:

1. _____
   _____

2. _____
   _____

3. _____
   _____

4. _____
   _____

5. _____
   _____

Step 4
Ace the Interview
Task 5: Interviewer Greeting

I have never experienced another human being.
I have experienced my impressions of them.

—Robert Anton Wilson

First Impressions with the Interviewer

There is an adage that says, "You only get one chance to make a first impression." There is a tremendous amount of truth to that adage. It is believed that a person develops an opinion about another person within ten to fifteen seconds after meeting them. That's right—seconds! Therefore, it is extremely important that you make an excellent first impression. There is nothing more important or personal to anyone than their name. You need to ensure that you know the correct pronunciation of the name of each person with whom you will be interviewing. Your initial handshake will also provide a first impression. Make sure that you make good eye contact and give the interviewer a good, firm handshake.

Action Steps for You:

1. Ensure that you have the interviewer's correct name.
2. Practice pronouncing the interviewer's name.
3. Look the interviewer in the eye when first meeting him or her.
4. Stand upright with squared shoulders.
5. Give the interviewer a firm handshake.
6. Smile when first meeting the interviewer.
7. Act as though you are excited to meet the interviewer.
8. Present yourself as though you are looking forward to the interview.

Additional Action Steps for You to Consider:

1. _____
   _____
2. _____
   _____
3. _____
   _____
4. _____
   _____

Step 4
Ace the Interview
Task 6: Interview Follow-Up

*Politics are almost as exciting as war, and quite as dangerous.
In war you can only be killed once, but in politics many times.*

—Winston Churchill

What to Do After the Interview

You have just completed the most successful interview that you have ever had. You and the interviewer were both comfortable and relaxed. You enjoyed your conversation and telling your SUPER™ stories. It appeared that you were the one to put the interviewer at ease. You truly controlled the interview! Now you are done, right? Wrong. Within the next twelve to twenty-four hours you need to send a thank-you note to each person with whom you interviewed. The note should be short but must reiterate a couple of your strong points. Mention something personal that you discussed during the interview. Indicate that you enjoyed talking with your interviewer(s) and that you look forward to talking with them again. This establishes your level of confidence and an expectation that you will be called back again.

Action Steps for You:

1. Close each interview by emphasizing your strengths.
2. Request permission to contact the interviewer with further questions.
3. Ensure that you have your interviewer's contact information.
4. Send all interviewers a handwritten thank-you note or e-mail.
5. Send thank-you notes to the people who helped you make contact.
6. Make a follow-up call to each interviewer to reiterate your interest.
7. Highlight additional points you may have missed during the interview.

Additional Action Steps for You to Consider:

1. _____

2. _____

3. _____

4. _____

5. _____

Sample Thank-You Letter

Your Name
Your Address
Your Phone Number and E-mail Address

The Interviewer's Name
The Interviewer's Title
The Interviewer's Company
The Interviewer's Address

Dear <*Put the interviewer's name here*>,

This is just a quick note to express my appreciation for your time and the opportunity to interview with you. Thank you.

I really enjoyed hearing your thoughts about <*Mention something the interviewer said.*>**. You truly gave me something to think about.**

I believe that my skills in the area of <*Mention one of your skills that can be applied to the position.*> **are a good match for this position. I am excited about having further conversations about applying my skills at** <*Put the company name here.*>**.**

I look forward to hearing from you.

Best regards,

Your name
Your phone number

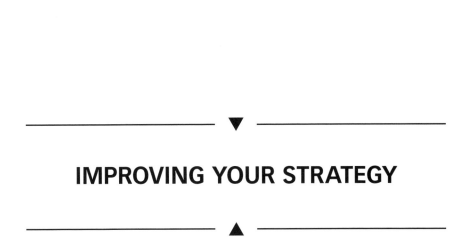

IMPROVING YOUR STRATEGY

Overview: Adjusting Your Strategy

There is a saying that goes, "The definition of insanity is doing the same thing over and over again, in the same way, and expecting different results." The objective of this chapter is to ensure that you are not proving this saying to be true.

You may have sent out a number of cover letters and resumes with no response. You may have had a number of interviews with no callbacks. The purpose of this chapter is to help you stop and reassess all aspects of your job-search campaign. I will show you the different areas of your campaign that you need to review to ensure that you are optimizing your job search.

You need to look at everything. There is no area that is too minor not to reexamine. For example, once when I reassessed my job search, I realized that I was concentrating on financial services companies, because that was where I had the most experience. I began looking at additional industries and was hired by a software development company. You should even take a second look at things like industry publications. You may learn about additional organizations that were not in your original list. These organizations may have publications to which you can subscribe. You need to ensure that you are subscribed to local publications, industry publications, and any publications that are specific to your skills and discipline.

You must review every aspect of your job-search strategy. Make adjustments to your personal network, company list, SUPER™ stories, and industry list. You should reexamine everything.

Once you have reexamined your plan, execute the new plan as often as possible until you are successful. Remember, there are always companies that are hiring. Your job is to use the techniques that I have provided you to find them. Use the interviewing techniques to get the position that you want.

You *will* be successful at advancing your career. You will then be ready to read the next chapter to learn about what you should do at your new job!

Step 1
Assess Plan Results
Task 1: Review Clubs and Associations

All activity isn't progress, just like all movement isn't forward.

—Wayne L. Anderson

Maximizing Association Contacts

By now you have been participating in a number of clubs and trade associations. Assess whether or not they have been helpful to your job search. Let's say you have been attending a large number of chamber of commerce business-networking sessions, but you have met very few people and have made hardly any contacts. You need to reassess whether or not to continue attending those sessions. In addition, you have just learned that there is a trade association in your industry that holds networking sessions; you need to immediately join that association and begin attending those events.

Keep in mind that performing the *activity* of attending is not enough. You must actively meet and talk with people. Let them know your situation. Ask them who else you should talk with if they cannot personally help you. Network, network, network!

Action Steps for You:

1. Determine if there are industry-related clubs to which you should belong.
2. Determine if there are other associations you should join.
3. Determine if there are other community organizations you should join.
4. Join additional organizations that will help your objective.

Additional Action Steps for You to Consider:

1. _____
   _____

2. _____
   _____

3. _____
   _____

4. _____
   _____

5. _____
   _____

Step 1
Assess Plan Results
Task 2 – Reassess the Market

The only limit to our realization of tomorrow
will be our doubts of today.

—Franklin D. Roosevelt

Reassessing the Market

You should not doubt yourself because you are not employed yet. Keep digging for sources of help so that you can realize your goal. Review your list of industries, companies, agencies, and job sites. Do more research to ensure that you have accessed as many as you can. Go to your local libraries and talk with the research librarians. Let them know what you are attempting to do. Show them the list that you have been working with to date. They are skilled at research and can help you dig up additional job-search gold nuggets that can help you.

Action Steps for You:

1. Determine if there are other industries you should pursue.
2. Determine if there are other companies you should pursue.
3. Determine if there are other recruiting agencies you should contact.
4. Ensure that you have access to all possible job websites.

Additional Action Steps for You to Consider:

1. _____
   _____
2. _____
   _____
3. _____
   _____
4. _____
   _____
5. _____
   _____

Step 2
Review Personal Information
Task 1: Review Cover Letter and Resume

Things should be made as simple as possible, but no simpler.

—Albert Einstein

Determining Why You Were Not Hired

You should contact any company that did not offer you a job and inquire about why you were not selected. Most companies are very willing to provide this information if they are approached in a professional manner. Sometimes you will find that they simply thought that your resume was too complicated or too long. Your resume and cover letter should be simple and easy to read. Hiring managers have to read lots of resumes. They are not going to spend a great deal of time on any resume or cover letter that is difficult to read. Review your resume and cover letter. There are an enormous number of sources that can help you create a professional resume. Make whatever adjustments are necessary to make your resume and cover letter more professional. For instance, you may look at a very long resume and consider removing positions that you held over ten years ago. You may find that the older positions demonstrate skills that do not pertain to the jobs you are currently seeking.

Action Steps for You:

1. Determine what you have learned.
2. Determine if cover letter should be adjusted.
3. Determine if your resume should be adjusted.
4. Make any necessary adjustments to your cover letter and resume.

Additional Action Steps for You to Consider:

1. _____
   _____
2. _____
   _____
3. _____
   _____
4. _____
   _____
5. _____
   _____

Step 2
Review Personal Information
Task 2: Assess Your Network

The most vital quality a soldier can possess is self-confidence.

—George S. Patton

Continuing to Grow Your Network

Regardless of how big your personal network is or has grown, it can be bigger. Look at all of the people in your network and make sure that you have systematically contacted each of them. Remember to ask each of them for up to three names of additional people that can help you. Contact anyone with whom you have become acquainted recently. Take them out for coffee or lunch. Ask them for the names of three people who can help you with your job search endeavor. Ask them about community events, association or club meetings, or any other type of event in which you should get involved. Develop the self-confidence to meet and talk with as many people as possible. You never know who will be the perfect person to assist you ... unless you talk with everyone!

Action Steps for You:

1. Determine what you have learned.
2. Determine if you should participate in any additional social networks.
3. Determine if there are more people you can contact.
4. Ensure that all people on your lists have been contacted.
5. Make the necessary adjustments to your network.

Additional Action Steps for You to Consider:

1. _____

2. _____

3. _____

4. _____

5. _____

Step 2
Review Personal Information
Task 3: Review your SUPER™ Stories

Never before have we had so little time in which to do so much.
—Franklin D. Roosevelt

The Effectiveness of Your SUPER™ Stories

Review how your SUPER™ stories were received during your interviews. Determine whether the stories were appropriate in answering the specific questions and whether you took advantage of each opportunity to tell your stories. Do you have enough SUPER™ stories? These stories are the most powerful tool that you have to move you ahead of the job-seeking pack. You need to ensure that your stories are perfect.

The best way to judge this is by both the verbal and nonverbal responses of your interviewers. For example, you may observe nonverbal responses such as the interviewer listening intently to the story or making a positive gesture such as nodding or smiling. You may observe verbal queues from the interviewer such as comments that the story was interesting or that the interview went by quickly—or that your time with them seemed more like a *conversation* rather than an interview. These are all signs that your stories were effective. Of course, the most positive sign is them asking you to return for another interview or, better yet, them offering you a job!

Action Steps for You:

1. Determine what you have learned from observing verbal and nonverbal responses.
2. Determine if your current SUPER™ stories should be adjusted.
3. Determine if you need additional SUPER™ stories.
4. Determine if you need to eliminate any SUPER™ stories.
5. Make the necessary adjustments to your SUPER™ stories.

Additional Action Steps for You to Consider:

1. _____
   _____
2. _____
   _____
3. _____
   _____
4. _____
   _____
5. _____
   _____

Step 2
Review Personal Information
Task 4: Review Your Research Techniques

*A good idea doesn't care who produces
it ... and neither should you.*

—Wayne L. Anderson

Improving Your Research Techniques

There may be many people who know more about how to conduct research than you do, like college professors, research librarians, corporate strategic planners, and, of course, college students. You need to determine if anyone in your personal network has excellent research skills. Seek them out and have them critique your research techniques. You can request their help via e-mail or telephone if you have this contact information. Generally, they will help you free of charge. Some may charge a nominal fee. Regardless, use any good ideas that they can provide you with. Try to contact and meet people with these skills who are not in your network. Make sure that you are not concerned about *who* provides you with a good idea ... just use it!

Action Steps for You:

1. Determine what you have learned from the research professionals.
2. Determine if your research techniques should be adjusted.
3. Make any adjustment necessary to improve your research techniques.

Additional Action Steps for You to Consider:

1. _____
   _____
2. _____
   _____
3. _____
   _____
4. _____
   _____
5. _____
   _____

Step 3
Make Plan Adjustments
Task 1: Reassess Your Opportunities

Old age is like a plane flying through a storm. Once you're aboard, there's nothing you can do.

—Golda Meir

Improving Your Opportunities

You need to ensure that you don't treat your plan like you treat old age, like something to be accepted just as it is. Your plan can be adjusted if it is not working in exactly the way you would like. You may think that you have exhausted every possible career opportunity. That is not true if you are still unemployed. Talk with local community workforce centers. They have counselors available to help you expand on the opportunities that may be open to you. Tap into your personal network and get ideas about other opportunities that may be related to your discipline or skills that you have not pursued yet. For example, an information technology (IT) client of mine was invited by a friend to attend a human resources conference. The IT person did not plan to attend since he knew he was not a human resources professional, but his friend convinced him to go anyway. At the conference, the IT professional learned about industries that were hiring that he did not originally have on his list. He was later hired in one of those industries.

Action Steps for You:

1. Assess what you have learned from talking to counselors and workforce professionals.
2. Determine if there are additional opportunities you should pursue.
3. Adjust your plan to include the new opportunities that you have found.

Additional Action Steps for You to Consider:

1. _____
_____
2. _____
_____
3. _____
_____
4. _____
_____
5. _____
_____

Step 3
Make Plan Adjustments
Task 2: Reassess the Industries

We must use time creatively—and forever realize
that the time is always hope to do great things.

—Martin Luther King Jr.

The Not-So-Obvious Industries

You may have spent most of your time researching the *obvious* industries that use your skills, but there may be many *not-so-obvious* industries that could also use your discipline and skills. For example, a research librarian generally works in a library; however, that person has a skill that could also be used in a corporate strategic planning organization. Spend some time talking with people in your personal network. Determine if there are other industries in which your skills can be used. Include those industries in your plan.

Action Steps for You:

1. Assess what you have learned from talking with your network.
2. Determine if there are additional industries you should pursue.
3. Adjust your plan to include these new industries.

Additional Action Steps for You to Consider:

1. _____
   _____
2. _____
   _____
3. _____
   _____
4. _____
   _____
5. _____
   _____

Step 3
Make Plan Adjustments
Task 3: Reassess the Company Types

*I usually make up my mind about a man in
ten seconds, and I very rarely change it.*

—Margaret Thatcher

The Not-So-Obvious Companies

Take time to think about other companies that can use your skills. Look for companies in industries that are growing. You should research any companies that have products and services that are needed today. Review newspapers, online articles, and publications for information about companies that are experiencing success. Are any of those companies missing from your list? Talk with people in your personal network. Ask them how their companies are doing. Ask them how their company's competition is doing. There are always companies that are hiring. You simply have to find out where they are and contact them. Ensure that you don't make up your mind too quickly about what is available to you.

Action Steps for You:

1. Assess what you have learned from your discussions and additional research.
2. List any additional companies and/or company types that you should pursue.
3. Adjust your plan to include new companies and/or company types.

Additional Action Steps for You to Consider:

1. _____
   _____

2. _____
   _____

3. _____
   _____

4. _____
   _____

5. _____
   _____

Step 3
Make Plan Adjustments
Task 4: Reassess Job-search websites

*Being a president is like riding a tiger. A man
has to keep on riding or he is swallowed.*

—Harry S. Truman

Updating Your Job-search websites

There are hundreds of job-search websites. Some are specific to particular skills, and some are more generic. Review the job sites where you have listed your resume and cover letter to determine if they are generic or specific sites. You may have adjusted your goals, industry list, and company list since visiting certain sites initially. If so, you may need to research any additional job-search websites that are available to you now that you have adjusted your plan. Talk with people in your personal network. Ask them about job-search websites that they would recommend or that they had success with. Ask a research librarian to help you put together a complete list of job-search websites. You need to keep riding the job-search tiger!

Action Steps for You:

1. Assess what you have learned from your network and research professionals.
2. Identify additional job-search websites you should utilize.
3. Determine whether the job-search websites you are currently using have been effective.
4. Adjust your plan to include new job-search websites.
5. Adjust your plan to eliminate ineffective job-search websites.

Additional Action Steps for You to Consider:

1. _____
   _____

2. _____
   _____

3. _____
   _____

4. _____
   _____

5. _____
   _____

Step 4
Re-Execute the Plan
Task 1: Making Contact

Am I not destroying my enemies when I make friends of them?
—Abraham Lincoln

Growing Your Personal Contacts

It is time to re-execute all of the techniques that we learned earlier, but now we are doing it with an updated plan. Remember, you want to create an unlimited supply of names and join many social networks. You need to contact individuals in your network, in companies, and in clubs and associations with whom you will eventually establish relationships. Make any necessary updates to all of your template notes, e-mails, and letters. You want to ensure that you are working with the most current communications.

Action Steps for You:

1.   Re-execute lead generation.
2.   Re-execute personal-note-card creation.
3.   Review and update your personal-letter template.
4.   Make contact with anyone new on your list.
5.   Set up personal appointments with anyone new on your list.
6.   Make post-appointment notes after meeting with your new contacts.

Additional Action Steps for You to Consider:

1. _____
   _____
2. _____
   _____
3. _____
   _____
4. _____
   _____
5. _____
   _____

Step 4
Re-Execute the Plan
Task 2: Power Networking

Do not let what you cannot do interfere with what you can do.

—John Wooden

The Art of Talking with People

Power networkers are people who are constantly meeting new people and talking with everyone they meet. They are good at the art of small talk. They know how to focus their conversations on others in order to develop long-lasting relationships. You can do this also. You talk with friends; you talk with family members; you talk with strangers. So, you can also talk with people in your network. You can ask for their help. You can tell them about your key product: you. You can tell them your elevator speech. You can ask them if you can practice your SUPER™ stories with them. These are all things that you *can* do!

Action Steps for You:

1. Continue practicing the art of small talk.
2. Identify and become a member of additional networking sites.
3. Participate in more association and organization functions.

Additional Action Steps for You to Consider:

1. _____
   _____
2. _____
   _____
3. _____
   _____
4. _____
   _____
5. _____
   _____

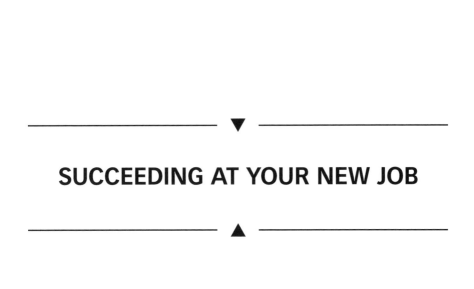

SUCCEEDING AT YOUR NEW JOB

Overview: Succeeding at Your New Job

Congratulations!

You have worked very hard to achieve success in advancing your career. You have landed what you believe to be a perfect job. You can take a deep breath and relax ... but only for a minute.

Why only a minute?

Well, most companies have a sixty- to ninety-day probation period. They use that time to determine if they made a wise decision in hiring you. If not, they have the right to terminate you without cause. Unfortunately, there are some people whose tenure is cut during the probation period. They never get a chance to demonstrate their real value to the company. There are generally some very simple techniques for surviving this period and going on to have a long career with your chosen company.

The purpose of this chapter is to provide you with some simple techniques to ensure you have a successful career in the company that you selected.

A good place to start is asking your new employer a very important question: "What would you expect to see me achieve in the next sixty to ninety days?" This will give you some insight as to where you need to focus your attention. You may be surprised that the answer to that question may describe items that are not in the job description they gave you, but this will provide important knowledge of what is expected of you. More important, it will let you know what the focal point of your activities must be.

It always amazes me how many people start their new jobs without spending any time learning more about their new companies. This is when your education about your new company should begin—and continue. There is a saying, "Enthusiasm is nothing but knowledge on fire!" I strongly believe this. To be an enthusiastic employee you must acquire as much knowledge about the company as possible. In this chapter, I will show you some techniques for acquiring this knowledge.

Step 1
Confirm Expectations
Task 1: New Job Description

*People with goals succeed because they
know where they're going.*

—Earl Nightingale

Understanding Your New Position

You had a goal to become reemployed, and you successfully achieved it. Now you have a new goal—to stay employed. One of the ways to achieve this goal is to be extremely clear as to what you are expected to do. An official, documented job description can help you to a certain extent, but what is written in the job description and what is *expected* may be two different things. You should ask your new employer, "What do you expect to see me achieve in the next sixty to ninety days?" You may not find the answer to that question anywhere in your job description. For example, your project management job description may contain a listing of all of the skills necessary to be a good project manager at your new company. But after discussing your new duties with your manager, you might also learn that you need to understand the technology that is being used on your assigned project. The technology knowledge that you are required to have is not documented anywhere in the job description that you were given, but this approach has helped make it clear where you should focus your attention.

Action Steps for You:

1. Obtain an official copy of your job description.
2. Inquire about your specific job functions.
3. Learn about expectations not documented in your job description.
4. Develop a strategy to meet or exceed your employer's expectations.

Additional Action Steps for You to Consider:

1. _____
_____
2. _____
_____
3. _____
_____
4. _____
_____
5. _____
_____

Step 1
Confirm Expectations
Task 2: Getting up to Speed

Nothing happens unless first a dream.

—Carl Sandburg

Advancing in Your New Company

I would guess that you dream of advancing steadily in your new company. One way to do this is to know as much about the company as possible. Your thirst for company knowledge should never go away. You should learn about all of the orientation and training programs available to you within the company. You should solicit the help of a human-resources professional in the company who can help you attain detailed information about the company. In addition, use the research techniques that you learned during your job search to uncover more in-depth knowledge about the company. For example, if it is a public company, your employer will have to file a 10-K report with the Securities and Exchange Commission (SEC). That document describes the company operations in detail. Obtain a copy of this document—and read it!

Action Steps for You:

1. Find out if your company has an orientation program.
2. Learn about sources of on-the-job training.
3. Learn about the corporate training process.
4. Learn about internal training opportunities and courses.
5. Learn about external opportunities for training.
6. Develop a personal training strategy to shorten your learning curve.

Additional Action Steps for You to Consider:

1. _____
   _____
2. _____
   _____
3. _____
   _____
4. _____
   _____
5. _____
   _____

Step 1
Confirm Expectations
Task 3: Role in Organization

*Every great and commanding moment in the annals
of the world is the triumph of some enthusiasm.*

—Ralph Waldo Emerson

Your Position in Your New Company

I am sure you are enthusiastic about your new company and your new position. However, you are obviously not the only person in the company, so you need to spend time understanding exactly where you are positioned in the organization. This will help you know who your peers are, who your superiors are, and, if you are a leader, who your subordinates are. It is important that you learn about the people within your department as well as the people in other departments with whom you interact.

Action Steps for You:

1. Learn where you are in the organizational chart.
2. Learn who you work with in your department.
3. Learn who you work with outside of your department.
4. Learn who uses your services within the company or department.
5. Learn who uses your services outside the company or department.

Additional Action Steps for You to Consider:

1. _____

2. _____

3. _____

4. _____

5. _____

Step 1
Confirm Expectations
Task 4: First Impression

A good plan is like a road map: it shows the final destination and usually marks the best way to get there.

—H. Stanley Judd

First Contact with Your New Coworkers

You may remember that you only get one chance to make a good first impression. You need a plan to make the right first impression in your new job. In addition to your interviewers, there are additional people with whom you will work each day. People will develop an impression about you within seconds of meeting you. When you were interviewing, you wanted to make sure the interviewer understood your skills. You may want your coworkers to understand your desire and ability to work with the team and share tasks.

Your coworkers will be observing the way you dress, your mannerisms, your attitude about meeting them, and so on. You need to first decide what you want that first impression to be. You must then develop a plan and practice the behaviors that will ensure that you present the impression that you want others to have of you.

Action Steps for You:

1. Create the impression you are *results oriented.*
2. Learn the company dress code.
3. Demonstrate that you accept responsibility. You can do this by volunteering to handle tasks for your manager or coworker.
4. Demonstrate that you have a positive attitude.
5. Demonstrate that you are approachable.
6. Demonstrate that you are trustworthy.
7. Demonstrate your willingness to learn.

Additional Action Steps for You to Consider:

1. _____
   _____
2. _____
   _____
3. _____
   _____
4. _____
   _____
5. _____
   _____

Step 1
Confirm Expectations
Task 5: Performance Criteria

What kills a skunk is the publicity it gives itself.

—Abraham Lincoln

Understanding Performance Expectations

It is extremely difficult to attain the success that you desire if you don't know what is expected of you. Performance expectations usually are developed at different levels. You will, of course, have performance criteria at your individual level, but your performance criteria are also going to be *tied* to criteria at both the department and company levels. It is important that you learn all of the priorities that exist to which your performance is connected. You will significantly increase your probability of success in your new company once you know and understand these priorities. These priorities become the bases for developing your personal success criteria.

Action Steps for You:

1. Learn your company's priorities.
2. Learn your department's priorities.
3. Learn your superior's success criteria (which are based on company and department priorities).
4. Learn your specific job's success criteria.
5. Establish a performance plan to accomplish these priorities and meet these criteria.

Additional Action Steps for You to Consider:

1. _____
   _____
2. _____
   _____
3. _____
   _____
4. _____
   _____
5. _____
   _____

Step 2
Develop an Internal Network
Task 1: Coaches and Mentors

*No meaningful aim will ever be attained if all
possible objections must first be overcome.*

—Wayne L. Anderson

Developing Mentors

There are many people within the company who can help you to be successful just as there were in your personal network. You already know from your job-search strategy the techniques for building personal and professional networks. You need to do the same thing internally within the company. You should develop an internal network that contains people who have been in the company for a long time. You should look for people who are in positions that you would like to attain; they can coach you on expected behaviors and how to be successful. In addition, they can mentor you on operations and processes that may not be documented anywhere.

I have had many mentors in the past who had a major impact on my success. Once, I approached an executive vice president in a financial services company in which I worked. I described for him my career aspirations and my desire to attain a position similar to his. I did not believe that a busy person at that level could ever have time to be a mentor, so I asked him if he had any suggestions as to whom I could approach as a mentor to help me. He immediately said yes and volunteered to be my mentor!

Find out if your company has a buddy system. This is generally a system where a new employee is assigned to a person or a team member (a buddy) who then helps the new employee to learn the way the company operates. That person is also available to answer any questions for the new person. Sometimes, they can simply direct the new employee to where to find the answers that they need. Buddy systems have proved very effective in helping new employees to become quickly oriented into companies.

Action Steps for You:

1. Determine if your company has a buddy system.
2. Introduce yourself to your buddy.
3. Determine if your company has a coaching or mentoring program.
4. Request a coach or mentor.
5. Introduce yourself to your coach or mentor.
6. Develop informal coaches and mentors if there is no formal program.

Additional Action Steps for You to Consider:

1. _____
   _____
2. _____
   _____
3. _____
   _____
4. _____
   _____
5. _____
   _____

Step 2
Develop an Internal Network
Task 2: Key Employees

*Not one of the things that you have done to date
will mean anything if you don't deliver.*

—Wayne L. Anderson

Learning about Successful People

The key to being successful in any organization is *delivering*. You need to deliver on your tasks; you need to deliver on your assignments; and most of all, you need to deliver on expectations. There are always people in any organization who have the reputation for being able to deliver on all of these things. You must find out who they are and determine what they do to be successful. You go to a doctor when you are sick because he or she is the best one to help you. Likewise, you go to an auto mechanic when your car needs servicing. In the same way, you must seek out the successful people at your new company to learn how to be successful there. Ask your coworkers and/or your mentor about who these people might be. These people may or may not become your mentors if they are successful but are not in positions that you wish to attain. They may be people with whom you simply meet once or twice to learn what they do. I learned a great deal from a person who was very successful in a company where I was employed. However, he worked in the pension benefits area, and I worked in the information technology area. He was very instrumental in helping me learn how to be successful in the company even though he was not one of my mentors.

Action Steps for You:

1. Learn who your department's successful people are.
2. Learn which of your peers from other areas are considered successful.
3. Learn the *key* management personnel.
4. Learn the *key* decision makers.
5. Develop relationships with these key people.

Additional Action Steps for You to Consider:

1. _____

2. _____

3. _____

4. _____

5. _____

Step 2
Develop an Internal Network
Task 3: Material Providers

The difference between a successful person and others is not a lack of strength, not a lack of knowledge, but rather in a lack of will.

—Vince Lombardi

Demonstrating Initiative and Making Connections

It is very likely that, whatever position you attain, you will need tools to do your job. It is not unusual for a person to "sit and wait" for someone to bring them the tools they need; that lack of will is generally noticed by people who make the staffing decisions. You need to demonstrate initiative and seek out the people who can provide the tools that you need. These are also good people to have in your internal network. And if they can't provide the materials you need, more often than not, they know where you can obtain them.

Action Steps for You:

1. Learn who provides equipment.
2. Learn who provides needed supplies.
3. Learn who makes decisions on supplying needed materials.
4. Ensure that you have the proper supplies needed to do your job.

Additional Action Steps for You to Consider:

1. _____
   _____
2. _____
   _____
3. _____
   _____
4. _____
   _____
5. _____
   _____

Step 3
Learn the Culture
Task 1: Company Values

*Here is a simple but powerful rule ... always
give people more than they expect to get.*

—Nelson Boswell

Using Company Values to Succeed

A company's personality is defined by its principles and values. These things help define the image that a company has in the marketplace, and they also help employees define themselves as members of that company. These principles and values provide guidance for the way the members of the company are expected to behave. You should take into account the company values when developing your personal performance strategy. Make sure that your strategy is designed to provide your new company with more than it is expecting of you.

Action Steps for You:

1. Learn the company's history.
2. Learn the company's overall goals.
3. Learn the company's values.
4. Learn the company's operating principles.
5. Get a copy of the employee handbook.
6. Develop a performance strategy based on the company's principles.
7. Include the company's values in your performance strategy.
8. Include the company's culture in your performance strategy.

Additional Action Steps for You to Consider:

1. _____
   _____

2. _____
   _____

3. _____
   _____

4. _____
   _____

5. _____
   _____

Step 3
Learn the Culture
Task 2: Professional Environment

Every problem contains the seed of its own solution.

—Norman Vincent Peale

Understanding Performance Evaluations

It is important to understand how you will be measured *before* you have a performance evaluation. This will help you prevent performance problems before you need a corrective solution. You need to determine if the company uses a 360-degree performance measurement technique. This is a technique in which your peers (both inside and outside of your department) and your subordinates, as well as your superiors, evaluate you. You should meet with each of these individuals if your company uses this method of evaluation. Learn what criteria each will be using to rate your performance.

Action Steps for You:

1. Determine how performance is measured.
2. Determine whether evaluations are completed by more than one person.
3. Determine *normal* work hours.
4. Find out if your company performs 360-degree evaluations.

Additional Action Steps for You to Consider:

1. _____
   _____
2. _____
   _____
3. _____
   _____
4. _____
   _____
5. _____
   _____

Step 4
Learn the Rules of Success
Task 1: Teams vs. Heroes

*Life is a grindstone. Whether it grinds us
down or polishes us up depends on us.*

—L. Thomas Holdcroft

Teamwork

It is possible that your previous success was based on your individual contribution. This is sometimes referred to as the hero reward system. In other words, you are highly rewarded for being an individual contributor (that is, a "hero") in your organization. An example of this is when you are given all of the credit for successfully completing a task even though a large number of people assisted you with it. This same behavior may be frowned upon in an organization that values teamwork, so it is important to understand *how* your company values success so that your approach to success is polished.

Action Steps for You:

1. Determine how your company defines success.
2. Determine how teams are rewarded.
3. Determine how individuals are rewarded.
4. Determine whether team results or individual results are most valued.
5. Develop a performance strategy depending on which is most valued.

Additional Action Steps for You to Consider:

1. _____
   _____

2. _____
   _____

3. _____
   _____

4. _____
   _____

5. _____
   _____

Step 4
Learn the Rules of Success
Task 2: Volunteering

Courage is doing what you're afraid to do. There can be no courage unless you're scared.

—Eddie Rickenbacker

Participating in the Community

Many companies have human resource policies that encourage employees to volunteer at outside organizations. The reason is that it develops an individual's critical organization and management skills in a noncritical environment. For example, you can volunteer to participate in the activities of a nonprofit organization where you learn such things as planning, organizing, control, and leadership. These are the main activities of a management professional. You might have never thought of volunteering in the past; initially, you might even be scared to do so. However, I strongly suggest that if your company has policies that encourage volunteering, you muster up the courage to participate. It can do tremendous things for your career.

Action Steps for You:

1. Determine the company policy on external volunteering.
2. Determine the company's views on internal volunteering.
3. Determine if volunteering will assist in your development.
4. Develop a strategy for volunteering if it is valued by company.
5. Develop a strategy for volunteering if it will assist in your development.

Additional Action Steps for You to Consider:

1. _____
   _____
2. _____
   _____
3. _____
   _____
4. _____
   _____
5. _____
   _____

Step 4
Learn the Rules of Success
Task 3: Unspoken Rules

When the student is ready the teacher will appear.

—Buddha

Learning Internal Success Techniques

When you are ready to be successful as a student of the new company, all of the information, techniques, and knowledge will be available to you, but you also need to develop a skill for learning through observation. The key behaviors necessary to be successful are not always documented. Through observation of how successful people perform, you can learn a great deal about the *unspoken* rules. In many cases, these rules are more important than the written ones. In addition, you should develop a skill for asking questions. You may read the written rules and then observe things being done differently. Learn why things are done the way they are. Sometimes strictly following the written rules can negatively impact your performance. For example, you may have a written rule stating that you should submit a status report each month, but then you observe that your coworkers submit one each week. You inquire about the increased frequency and learn the rules were changed a number of years ago, but no one updated the documentation! Be a good student. Learn how the successful people became successful.

Action Steps for You:

1. Observe how others behave.
2. Ask questions about why things are done a certain way.
3. Learn how undocumented processes work.
4. Learn who possesses the most influence.
5. Develop a strategy to learn and understand the unspoken (and unwritten) rules.

Additional Action Steps for You to Consider:

1. _____
   _____

2. _____
   _____

3. _____
   _____

4. _____
   _____

5. _____
   _____

Step 4
Learn the Rules of Success
Task 4: Manager/Employee Relationship

*The most valuable of all talents is that of never
using two words when one will do.*

—Thomas Jefferson

Developing a Good Working Relationship

Remember the saying, "We have two ears and one mouth for a reason." You need to develop a skill for providing fewer words with your mouth than you hear with your ears. In other words, develop strong listening skills. You should use those skills to develop a good working relationship with your new management team. It is important to keep in mind that they reached their level in the organization because they have some of the skills that you require to be successful. The best way to learn and develop those skills is to develop a strong working relationship with your manager. The most effective way to achieve that goal is to listen and learn.

Action Steps for You:

1. Hold brief meetings with your new manager.
2. Learn your manager's management style.
3. Determine common ground between you and manager.
4. Make your manager aware of your work style.
5. Develop a strategy to integrate your work style with your manager's style.
6. Listen closely to the information that your new manager provides you with.
7. Learn what you need to do to be successful at the company.
8. Learn how to help your manager to be successful in his or her job.

Additional Action Steps for You to Consider:

1. _____
   _____
2. _____
   _____
3. _____
   _____
4. _____
   _____
5. _____
   _____

Congratulations!

You have successfully obtained the tools and strategies that will propel you ahead in your job search endeavor. You will be able to advance ahead of the other people competing for the same jobs that you are pursuing.

I constantly talk with my coaching clients about competing with other job seekers. I like to use the analogy of a horse race. There are times when the winner of a horse race can command a purse that is up to ten times that of the runner-up. However, as we all know, the second horse does not always lose by ten lengths—sometimes it is just by a nose! I endeavored to arm you with tools and techniques that could help you win the job … sometimes by just a little bit.

That little bit could be the fact that you have learned organization techniques. Or that you have learned to look at all aspects of yourself and take an inventory of your skills and abilities, knowing that many job seekers bypass this step. You learned what items in your personal inventory will be a tremendous help to achieving your goal.

In addition to being organized, we covered how to develop and execute an effective job-search strategy. You now know that it is extremely important that you have a strategy. You learned that if you don't know where you're going, any road will get you there. So we discussed developing a strategy, creating a plan from that strategy, and identifying techniques for executing the plan.

The chapter on executing your plan also discussed the concept of networking. This is making contact with people who can help you be successful in finding a job. The people you know and the people they know are important to your success. We discussed that making contact is only the first step. It is also imperative for you to know *how* to make contact and what to do once you have made contact.

Executing your plan also requires telling people about yourself when you are networking. Therefore, we covered the concept of developing the

"You" brand. Companies establish a brand for their products; you are doing the same thing. The only difference is your product is you!

There are situations in which you don't always have a lot of time to communicate your product. For these instances, you will develop an elevator speech to communicate your key skills in a short period of time.

In the case of an interview, you have more time to communicate your skills. You learned the techniques of developing and delivering SUPER™ stories. This approach will help you to create memorable pictures of you and your major skills in the minds of your interviewers. These pictures connect you with potential jobs in a meaningful way. You also learned that using this technique helps you, the interviewee, to control the interview.

So, your control of the interview will help you to get the job. Great! Once you have the job, what should you do to keep it? The final chapter gave you the methods and strategies for keeping your new job. Most of all, you also learned how to be successful and grow in your new position.

I am extremely proud of you!

Now go out and get re-employed!

References

Government Websites

Bureau of Labor Statistics (http://www.bls.gov)

"The Bureau of Labor Statistics is the principal fact-finding agency for the Federal Government in the broad field of labor economics and statistics. The BLS is an independent national statistical agency that collects, processes, analyzes, and disseminates essential statistical data to the American public, the US Congress, other Federal agencies, State and local governments, business, and labor. The BLS also serves as a statistical resource to the Department of Labor."[1] You will find a wealth of information on this website. For example, it can help you:

determine the areas with the highest unemployment;
understand national and local employment statistics;
determine job-opening statistics;
see trends in pay and benefits statistics; and more.

US Census Bureau (http://www.census.gov)

"The Census Bureau serves as the leading source of quality data about the nation's people and economy. We honor privacy, protect confidentiality, share our expertise globally, and conduct our work openly. We are guided on this mission by our strong and capable workforce, our readiness to innovate, and our abiding commitment to our customers."[2] On this site you can find:

the number of people in a particular area of the country;

1   Source: Bureau of Labor Statistics website
2   Source: US Census Bureau website

247

the number and types of companies in a particular area;
the growth trends in particular areas of the country;
income levels in various areas of the country; and more.

USAJOBS (http://www.usajobs.gov)
This is a government website that informs you about jobs that are available within the federal government.

Quote Websites

Many of the quotes contained in this book are from:

BrainyQuote (http://www.brainyquote.com/)
ThinkExist.com (http://en.thinkexist.com/)

About the Author

Wayne L. Anderson is an executive-leadership coach for the Leadership Science Institute, LLC (LSI), which he founded. LSI is a leadership-development, training, and mentoring organization that is focused on building strong and effective leaders. In addition, Wayne is the president and chief strategist at Anderson Professional Systems Group, LLC, (APSG), an IT-management-consulting company that he also founded. APSG specializes in improving the value of businesses through effective use of the information-technology organization.

Wayne has over thirty years in the business world. He is a senior executive with an equal blend of technical, business, and managerial skills developed during experience with several Fortune-500 companies. He works with senior-level executives and corporations to further their long- and short-range employment goals. He provides extensive experience in managing multi-million-dollar budgets and large professional staffs. Wayne also possesses the unique ability to help his clients to attract, retain, develop, and motivate outstanding management and professional personnel.

He is the author of *Unwrapping the CIO: Demystifying the Chief Information Officer Position* and *Powerful People Are Powerful IT Professionals*. Wayne is the keynote speaker at a number of professional and academic events. He is an adjunct professor in business and management at Front Range Community College in Westminster, Colorado. In addition, he coaches executive leaders and business professionals on the techniques necessary to be successful in their positions.

You may connect with Wayne through his professional network on LinkedIn.com (http://www.linkedin.com/in/ciounwrapped), and you may e-mail him at wayne@leadershipscienceinstitute.com. Feel free to visit Wayne's website at http://www.leadershipscienceinstitute.com

Wayne resides in Colorado with his wife, Pam.

Index